The
HIDDEN PLACES
of
WARWICKSHIRE AND
THE WEST MIDLANDS

Edited by
Barbara Vesey

ii

Published by:
Travel Publishing Ltd
7a Apollo House, Calleva Park
Aldermaston, Berks, RG7 8TN

ISBN 1-902-00724-7

© Travel Publishing Ltd 1999

First Published: *1990*
Second Edition: *1995*
Third Edition: *1999*

Regional Titles in the Hidden Places Series:

Cambridgeshire & Lincolnshire	Channel Islands
Cheshire	Cornwall
Devon	Dorset, Hants & Isle of Wight
Essex	Gloucestershire
Heart of England	Highlands & Islands
Kent	Lake District & Cumbria
Lancashire	Norfolk
Northeast Yorkshire	Northumberland & Durham
North Wales	Nottinghamshire
Peak District	Potteries
Somerset	South Wales
Suffolk	Surrey
Sussex	Thames & Chilterns
Warwickshire & W Midlands	Welsh Borders
Wiltshire	Yorkshire Dales

National Titles in the Hidden Places Series:

England	Ireland
Scotland	Wales

Printing by: Nuffield Press, Abingdon
Maps by: © MAPS IN MINUTES ™ (1998)
Line Drawings: Roz Hackney
Editor: Barbara Vesey
Cover : Clare Hackney

Born in 1961, Clare was educated at West Surrey College of Art and Design as well as studying at Kingston University. She runs her own private water-colour school based in Surrey and has exhibited both in the UK and internationally. The cover is taken from an original water-colour of Chesterton Windmill, near Harbury.

FOREWORD

The Hidden Places series is a collection of easy to use travel guides taking you, in this instance, on a relaxed but informative tour through Warwickshire and the West Midlands, a region with a history stretching back to the Bronze Age but which, in more recent times, played a crucial role in the political and industrial evolution of the UK. Warwickshire, of course, is the foundation of Shakespeare's literary heritage and also possesses some of the country's most beautiful countryside including many hidden places. Our books contain a wealth of interesting information on the history, the countryside, the towns and villages and the more established places of interest in the county. But they also promote the more secluded and little known visitor attractions and places to stay, eat and drink many of which are easy to miss unless you know exactly where you are going.

We include hotels, inns, restaurants, public houses, teashops, various types of accommodation, historic houses, museums, gardens, garden centres, craft centres and many other attractions throughout Warwickshire and the West Midlands, all of which are comprehensively indexed. Most places have an attractive line drawing and are cross-referenced to coloured maps found at the rear of the book. We do not award merit marks or rankings but concentrate on describing the more interesting, unusual or unique features of each place with the aim of making the reader's stay in the local area an enjoyable and stimulating experience.

Whether you are visiting the area for business or pleasure or in fact are living in the counties we do hope that you enjoy reading and using this book. We are always interested in what readers think of places covered (or not covered) in our guides so please do not hesitate to use the reader reaction forms provided to give us your considered comments. We also welcome any general comments which will help us improve the guides themselves. Finally if you are planning to visit any other corner of the British Isles we would like to refer you to the list of other *Hidden Places* titles to be found at the rear of the book.

CONTENTS

1 Birmingham and North Warwickshire

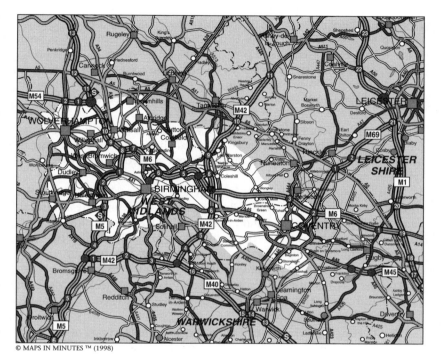

© MAPS IN MINUTES ™ (1998)

The extreme northwest of Warwickshire, dominated by the major West Midlands cities of Birmingham and Coventry, often gets overlooked by visitors but repays a closer look. It is an area rich in natural beauty, with a wealth of beautiful gardens, some excellent museums and historic buildings, and a long and distinguished industrial and cultural heritage.

BIRMINGHAM

Birmingham is perceived by many who don't know it well as a maze of glass-and-steel buildings and other modern monstrosities. It rewards a visit many times over, however, in its wealth of museums, marvellous public spaces, historic buildings and wealth of sights, sounds and attractions. It is a city with a rich and varied industrial history taking in everything from the first steam engine to button, buckles, clocks and chocolate.

The Domesday Book reports that in the survey of 1086, the hamlet of Birmingham was among the least prosperous manors in the area, and valued it at £1. Geography played a role in Birmingham's rise to fortune, as it was a dry site with a good supply of water and important routes which converged at Deritenford across the little River Rea. There was also easy access to coal, iron and timber stores from the nearby Black Country.

Peter de Bermingham obtained rights of trading in a Market Charter granted in 1166 by King Henry II. By the mid-16th century there were some 1,500 people living in 200 homes, as well as one main street and a number of side-streets, markets for grain and livestock, and mills for tanning. Already the smiths were selling their knives and all manner of tools throughout England. Lorimers and nailers were also part of the town's growing industries.

This growth was helped along by the demands of the Parliamentarians, who during the Civil War needed a virtually endless supply of swords, pikes and armour. So it was that Birmingham emerged with a strong reputation as a metal centre.

By the 1750s the population had swelled to over 20,000, and by the time of the Industrial Revolution Birmingham had become the industrial, commercial and cultural capital of the Midlands. This was due in large part to the industriousness of the native 'Brummies'. Today this tradition continues, enhanced by the influxes of peoples of differing nationalities and cultures, each adding their own unique gifts and talents to the mix.

The city has had many famous sons and daughters. In Birmingham's parish **Church of St Martin** there are memorials to the two Lords of the Manor, the de Berminghams.

The Birmingham Symphony Orchestra, recognised as one of the finest in the world, perform a regular season in the classical Roman-inspired **Town Hall**, built by Joseph Hansom, of hansom cab fame , and E Welch. Mendelssohn gave several organ recitals here.

Sporting facilities abound in Birmingham The famous **Belfry Golf Course** in Lichfield Road, Wishaw, near Sutton Coldfield is open to the public. There are public squash courts at the Birmingham Squash Rackets Centre in Rotton Park, Edgbaston and at Wyndley Leisure Centre, Clifton Road, Sutton Coldfield to name but two. Also at Wyndley Centre are swimming and many other sports activities.

Soccer clubs Aston Villa, Birmingham City and, not far away, Wolverhampton Wanderers, West Bromich Albion and Walsall all provide opportunities to find a good match in the season. Edgbaston of course, is synonymous with cricket, both county and test.

There are no fewer than 6,000 acres of parkland and open space in Birmingham. **Cannon Hill Park** in Edgbaston is one particular highlight. It has 80 acres of flower and ornamental gardens. Also in Edgbaston, on

Westbourne Road, the **Botanical Gardens** comprise 15 acres and boast a Tropical House with lily pond, banana and cocoa trees, the Palm House, Orangery, National Bonsai Collection, Cactus House and the gardens themselves, filled with rhododendrons, azaleas and a good collection of trees. **Birmingham Nature Centre**, not far away on Pershore Road, has British and European wildlife - including wallaby, fallow deer, otters and reptiles - in indoor and outdoor enclosures resembling as closely as possible the creatures' native habitats. At **Edgbaston Reservoir** there is every kind of water recreation visitors could wish for.

The focus for shopping is New Street, Corporation Street, and the Bull Ring Shopping Centre; coming away from these areas there are some very attractive Victorian arcades which house the smaller speciality shops. Birmingham is traditionally a centre of jewellery - indeed there is an 18th-century church in St Paul's Square known simply as The Jewellers Church. The **Jewellery Quarter Discovery Centre** is a good place to start if you'd like to learn more about times past and present in the Birmingham jewellery trade. It is located on Vyse Street, centred round the preserved workshops of Smith & Pepper, still much as they were at the turn of the century. You will find jewellers still abound, especially in the Hockley area. Gunsmiths are also to be found here, another craft for which Birmingham is renowned.

Birmingham is also outstanding for its indoor markets. It is a tradition that stems back to the first Market Charter some 800 years ago. You will find them close to St Martin's church. The Rag Market is the place to spot a bargain, whereas the Bull Ring Open Air Market and the Bull Ring Centre Market Hall deal in anything from food to household goods. Monday is the day to go looking for antiques in the Rag Market.

One would expect a city as flourishing as Birmingham to be a natural centre for theatre, and it is. **The Hippodrome** was once a music hall but it has become one of the leading opera houses in the country as well as a centre for musicals, international ballet and some wonderful pantomimes. The theatre was restored in the not too distant past and, without having lost any of the magic of an old theatre, has become one of the best equipped anywhere.

More renovation and rebuilding has gone on to produce the **Birmingham Repertory Theatre**, which has become celebrated for major musicals, comedies and classics.

The city's Annual Jazz Festival brings together big name starts from the world of jazz. The week's activities include hundreds of performances including open-air gigs and street-corner jam sessions.

The **Museum and Art Gallery** in Chamberlain Square represents the 17th, 18th, and 19th centuries, including the world's finest examples of works by the Pre-Raphaelites. The contemporary art of sculpture is also well represented. Costume, silver, textiles and ceramics as well as works of ethnography from around the world, among which is a large and rare copper Buddha from Sultangani.

Public works of art include the murals in **Colmore Circus**. One of these depicts a Civil War battle, another the Industrial Revolution. **Holloway Circus** has an enormous mural measuring 85 feet by 14 feet and showing The Horse Fair of 1908.

The Barber Institute at Birmingham University houses an excellent collection of paintings and sculptures. There is a wealth of Impressionist pieces, as well as the work of European masters.

Birmingham's newest museum is **Soho House**, a handsome Georgian building which has been carefully restored to its original elegance. Former home of the pioneering industrialist Matthew Boulton, James Watt's business partner and founder of the Soho Mint, who lived here from 1766 to 1809, it contains some of his original furnishings. Displays relate the story of the man and his times, and offer a chance to see some of the fruits of Boulton's nearby factory - buttons and buckles, ormolu clocks and vases, silver and Sheffield plate tableware - where he and Watt developed the steam engine.

Soho House, Birmingham

There are some 2,000 listed buildings in Birmingham, dating from the Elizabethan, Jacobean, Georgian and Victorian periods. The 1879 neo-Renaissance **Council House** is an impressive testament to the city's success and achievements. The Curzon Street **Goods Station** is a colonnaded building dating from 1838. Built by Philip Hardwick, its Ionic portico celebrates the wonder of the then-new railway industry.

Let it not be forgotten that Birmingham is a city of canals. **Gas Street Basin** in the centre of Birmingham marks the hub of a 2,000 mile canal network. Canals run from here to Liverpool, Nottingham, London and Gloucester. The Basin also has quiet towpaths made for quiet strolling. The Tourist Information Centre has a great deal of information on pleasant walks that can be taken along Birmingham's extensive network of waterways, taking in many historic buildings, locks, factories and cottages along the way, as well as the plants and wildlife who make their home here.

Sarehole Mill in Cole Bank Road in Hall Green is Birmingham's only working water mill. The former childhood haunt of J R R Tolkein (author of The Hobbit and Lord of the Rings), it was used as a flour mill and also to roll and smooth metal needed during the Industrial Revolution. The present buildings are mainly Georgian, having been rebuilt in the 1760s, were in use, commercially, right up to 1919. The mill then fell into disrepair, though it was later carefully restored to working order. Visitors have the opportunity to see the interior, and one of the two waterwheels is regularly operated, subject to the availability of water in the millpond. The process of grinding corn can be followed on all three floors of the mill, whilst in the adjoining building a reconstruction of a blade-grinding workshop shows how the mill was partially converted to industrial use in the 18th century. The granary contains displays on local agriculture and rural life, illustrated by farm and craft tools, machinery and horse-drawn vehicles. The engine house was added in the 1850s and contained a steam engine that supplemented the water power from the River Cole. The original engine was removed many years ago, but one of similar type was installed in the 1970s when the building was restored.

Another nearby attraction well worth a visit is **Castle Bromwich Hall Gardens,** on Chester Road, about four miles east of the city centre. This boasts a collection of plants grown here in the 18th century, including historic herbs and vegetable species, shrubs and border plants, in a classic formal layout popular in the 1700s. Guided tours available.

Like many other large English cities, Birmingham is a network of neighbourhoods, like smaller towns within the larger metropolis, each with its unique atmosphere, attractions and traditions.

AROUND BIRMINGHAM

ASTON   MAP 1 REF C3
2 miles N of Birmingham off the A34

Aston Hall was one of the last great Jacobean country houses to be built in England. Like Hatfield House and Blickling Hall, it has a highly intricate plan and a dramatic skyline of turrets, gables and chimneys. It is also administered by Birmingham Museum and Art Gallery, who have done much to make it a memorable place to visit. The house was built between 1618 and 1635 by Sir Thomas Holte, and remained the seat of the Holte family

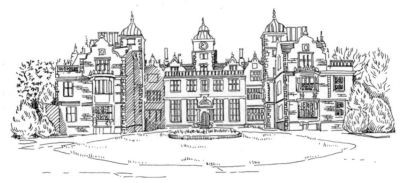

Aston Hall, Aston

until it was sold off in 1817. King Charles I came to Aston Hall in 1642, at the beginning of the Civil War, and it was later besieged and sacked by Parliamentarian soldiers. Much Jacobean decorative work of high quality still survives, especially the moulded plasterwork. The house has a most wonderful staircase and Long Gallery.

In the 14th century church at Aston, Ralph Arden, an early ancestor of William Shakespeare, is moulded in effigy, and there is also a handsome black marble and alabaster memorial to the 17th century knight Sir Edward Devereux , as well as of two unidentified armoured knights.

ASHOVER   MAP 1 REF C2
8 miles N of Birmingham off the B4138

Signposted from Streetly, north of Birmingham, the garden at **25 Burnett Road** is well worth a visit. Comprising one-third of an acre, it is a plant-lover's garden with cottage-style mixed plantings planned for year-round interest, with bulbs, shrubs and herbaceous plants. Owners Jackie and

Martin Harvey also offer visitors cream teas. Part of The National Gardens Scheme Charitable Trust (for information about opening times, ring 01926 624304).

KINGSBURY
MAP 4 REF D2
7 miles NE of Birmingham off the A4097

Kingsbury Water Park boasts over 600 acres of country park, with loads to see and do, including birdwatching, picnic sites, nature trails, fishing and good information centre. There is also a cosy cafe and special unit housing the park's shop and exhibition hall. Also with the park, **Broomey Croft Children's Farm** makes for an enjoyable and educational day out for all the family, with a wealth of animals housed in renovated early 19th-century farm buildings.

NETHER WHITACRE
MAP 4 REF D3
9 miles NE of Birmingham off the B4098

This very attractive village dates back to the Domesday Book. It is just as handy for those touring Nuneaton (six miles away), Tamworth (three miles distant) and Kingsbury (two and half miles away).

A true jewel hidden away for travellers to find, enjoy, and return to again and again, **The Dog Inn** occupies a former farmer's cottage dating

The Dog Inn, Dog Lane, Nether Whitacre
Nr Coleshill, Warwickshire B46 2DU Tel: 01675 481318.

back nearly 500 years. It became a licensed premises in the early 19th century - a list of the licensees can be seen written on one of the pub's beams. The conker tree adjacent to the pub has a preservation order, as it dates back over 600 years. Every October the pub celebrates a special Conker night. With over 20 years experience in the trade, Clare and Roy Black became the leaseholders here in 1995. The food available is of a high quality, with steaks and fish dishes a speciality; there are also six homemade specials daily for lunch, and another six for dinner. The excellent ales on offer include Bass, Brew XI and a guest ale, plus Bass Mild, Caffrey's, Guinness, and draught lagers and ciders. There is also a fine wine list. Out back there's a lovely cottage garden. The hospitality and atmosphere in this welcoming establishment are hard to beat. In addition planning permission has been granted to convert the outside barns into letting rooms.

YARDLEY   MAP 1 REF C4
2 miles E of Birmingham off the A45/A4040

Blakesley Hall is Birmingham's finest Elizabethan building. Built in 1590, it is an extremely attractive timber-framed farmhouse which has been carefully restored. Owned by Birmingham Museum and Art Gallery, its rich, decorative framing and jettied first and second floors reflect the wealth of its Elizabethan owner and builder, Richard Smallbroke, one of the leading

Blakesley Hall, Yardley

merchants of the time. A diminutive and rare Long Gallery survives, whilst in Smallbroke's bedroom the original wall paintings were uncovered in 1950. Some of the 12 rooms are furnished to look as they did in 1684, when an inventory of the house's contents was drawn up.

Old Yardley village is one of Birmingham's outstanding conservation areas. Within walking distance of Blakesley Hall, it is truly remarkable for its medieval church and Trust School. Of particular note are the pretty Georgian cottages.

FILLONGLEY   MAP 4 REF E3
10 miles E of Birmingham off the B4102

This very scenic village has many lovely old cottages set amid lovely rural Warwickshire countryside.

The Cottage Inn, which dates back to the mid-18th century, was totally refurbished throughout in 1996. Retaining a style and character all its own, this traditional country pub boasts a patio area and gardens where customers can enjoy a hearty meal and a quiet drink when the weather is fine. The interior is stylish and welcoming, with a wealth of memorabilia

The Cottage Inn, Blackhall Lane, Fillongley, Warwickshire CV7 8EG
Tel: 01676 540599.

adorning the walls. The good range of ales on offer includes Boddingtons, Marstons Pedigree and a guest ale. The menu is extensive, offering a range of traditional favourites such as Sunday roast, bangers and mash and fish and chips to more innovative dishes such as pasta with pesto rosso, beef or vegetable chilli and Chinese stir fry, all prepared and cooked to a high standard of excellence. Open for lunch and evening Monday to Saturday, all day Sunday.

CORLEY MOOR   MAP 4 REF E4
10 miles E of Birmingham off the A45

Corley Moor is a pretty little village boasting some picturesque scenery and handsome architecture. **The Bull & Butcher** is a convivial and charming public house in buildings dating back to the mid-18th century. Once comprising a slaughterhouse and butcher's shop as well as a pub (the first two are now closed, though the old butcher's shop stills stands adjacent), it is run with conscientious attention by licensees Nick and Diane, who came here in 1995. Very popular for its quality food and ale, the pub is open lunchtimes and evenings daily, with food available from 12-2 p.m. and 6-9.30 p.m. The menu is outstanding, its variety encompassing dishes to suit every taste, all home-prepared and home-cooked. There are also changing daily specials. The range of excellent ales available includes Worthington Smooth, Brew XI, Bass and Abbot Ale, plus mild, draught lagers, ciders and Guinness. Nick and Diane work hard to maintain the traditions and feel of an old English country pub, as the decor and ambience attest.

The Bull & Butcher, Common Lane, Corley Moor
Warwickshire CV7 8AQ Tel: 01676 540241.

HAMPTON-IN-ARDEN
6 miles SE of Birmingham off the A452

MAP 1 REF D4

This lovely village in the heart of the ancient forest of Arden is said to have been the inspiration for the setting of Shakespeare's As You Like It. The delightfully picturesque streets are lined with pretty ornamented cottages. The **Church of St Mary and St Bartholomew** has a perpendicular tower which, until 1643, was topped by a spire. There is a Norman and 13th century nave and a Norman chancel. The chancel is entered through an arch adorned with carved heads, and has some medieval blue-and-white tiles in the flooring. **Hampton Manor House** has a most interesting pyramid clock tower.

Situated on the main street of this picturesque village, **Naughty Nick's** is a tea shop which also accommodates the village's heritage centre. The tea rooms are situated in what was once the village bakery, in a brickbuilt building dating back to the 17th century. This cosy area seats 12 inside, with space for another 12 outdoors on fine days. The menu includes breakfasts and traditional favourites such as freshly made sandwiches and jacket

**Naughty Nick's, The Old Bakery, 6 High Street, Hampton-in-Arden
Warwickshire B92 0AA Tel: 01675 443330.**

potatoes, as well as a wonderful selection of mouth-watering cakes, pies and other puddings. The heritage centre within the tea room boasts old pictures of the village, with details of the village's past and present, how it has changed and what has remained the same. The tea room is open Monday-Saturday 8 a.m.-5.30 p.m. Just next door, Nick's mum and dad, Maureen and Malcolm, run the village shop, a charming old-fashioned place which hearkens back to a time when the village shop was the true heart of village life.

There has been an inn on the site of the **White Lion** in Hampton-in-Arden for over 600 years. The lovely church opposite is mentioned in the Domesday Book. This former farmhouse is constructed, as was common at the time, from ship's timbers - however, in this case the timbers were coming 'back home', having been native Warwickshire oaks when they started out life. Steeped in history, this traditional English country inn offers real hospitality and a warm welcome. Past winner of Solihull pub of the year, this family-run inn has a reputation for good food and ales, and is popular with both locals and visitors. The inn boasts CAMRA award-winning beers, as well as good bar snacks and home-made sandwiches. The recently expanded and refurbished Spiral Drive Restaurant to the rear of the inn offers delicious Modern English cuisine with a Continental accent; fresh fish dishes are a speciality. For those wishing to prolong their stay in this picturesque part of the county, there are also eight ensuite rooms here, very comfortable and traditional in style.

The White Lion, The High Street, Hampton-in-Arden
Warwickshire B92 0AA Tel: 01675 442833 Fax: 01675 443168.

BALSALL COMMON
8 miles SE of Birmingham off the A452

MAP 1 REF D4

This handsome Warwickshire village boasts **Balsall Common Gardens**, a collection of individual private gardens open to the public as part of a gardening scheme (telephone 01676 533143 for details). Maps are available for each garden. Featured gardens include The Bungalow in Table Oak Lane (2 acres of mixed borders, pond and lawn), Firs Farm in Windmill Lane (½ acre garden comprising walled garden, formal bedding and mixed borders), Meriglen, also in Windmill Lane (¾ acre mixed borders, small woodland), The Pines in Hodgetts Lane (1½ acre formal garden with an avenue of flowering trees, series of small gardens, herb garden and rose walk), Silver Trees Farm in Balsall Street (1½ acres, with mixed borders, orchard, bog area, woodland garden, large formal pond), Fen End House in Fen End (1-acre garden, with lawns interspersed with borders comprising formal and informal planting schemes), White Cottage Farm in Holly Lane (1½ acres of cottage garden, mixed borders, pond, sunken garden), and 32 Wootton Green Lane (lawns, water features, greenhouses). Cream teas are on offer at White Cottage and Silver Trees Farm.

Balsall Common is also home to **La Pergola International Restaurant**. Owner Lotfi Saidi brought with him a wealth of experience in the restaurant trade when he took over this establishment some three years ago. He has made it a very popular place to eat, with a high standard for service and quality. This beautifully decorated establishment is cosy and intimate, though it seats up to 56 (booking advised at weekends). There is

**La Pergola International Restaurant, 376 Kenilworth Road
Balsall Common, Warwickshire CV7 7ER Tel: 01676 533308.**

a comfortable seating area for pre- or after dinner drinks in this licensed premises. Lotfi's international team of Tunisian, Italian, Portuguese and English staff have created an innovative and creative menu. With an accent on a blend of all these different traditions, the menu offers a tempting range of fish, beef, poultry and pasta dishes. Fresh fish dishes are the house speciality. The puddings are a real treat; the only difficulty will be deciding which to choose from the excellent range on offer. Open: Monday-Friday lunch 12-2.30; every evening 6.30-10.30.

The farm buildings that make up **Old Lodge Farm Antiques and B&B** in Balsall Common date back in parts to 1795; the main barn, where the antiques are displayed, was built in 1820. Owners John and Diane Wright have lived here for four years, and have 15 years' experience in the antiques trade. They buy as well as sell, as they are always keen to add to their collection of 18th and 19th century antiques and 20th century pieces. They specialise mainly in furniture, ceramics, china, curios and collectibles.

**Old Lodge Farm Antiques and B&B, Kenilworth Road
Balsall Common, Warwickshire CV7 7EY Tel: 01676 535282.**

All the pieces are nicely arranged for browsing at leisure, and there is something to suit every pocket. The outbuildings are being refurbished bit by bit; when these refurbishments are complete there will be 3,000 square feet of display area. The old stable buildings are also being renovated, to create two ensuite rooms for bed and breakfast accommodation. These ground-floor rooms will sleep two and three people respectively. Open: Monday-Wednesday-Friday 11 a.m.-4 p.m., Saturday-Sunday 10 a.m.-5p.m., and by appointment.

MERIDEN
MAP 4 REF D4
9 miles SE of Birmingham off the A45

Packington Hall in Meriden has magnificent gardens laid out in 1750 by 'Capability' Brown. The lawns are dotted with clumps of azaleas and rhododendrons, as well as specimen trees, and run down to the 18 acre Hall Pool. The more formal area around the house has recently been replanted. (Please telephone 01926 624304 for opening times and other details.)

Set in attractive wooded grounds, **Somers Wood Caravan and Camping Park** is a delightful family-run facility which is open all year round. The park offers 48 hard and soft standing pitches and is well provided with electric hook-ups and water points. The newly constructed timber amenities block includes heated showers and water, toilets, and dishwashing sinks. A laundry service is also available. Welcoming to all, it stands adjacent to Stonebridge Golf Centre and the Somers Coarse Fishery, with the Pakington Trout Fishery only a short distance away, making it especially

**Somers Wood Caravan and Camping Park, Somers Road, Meriden
Warwickshire CV7 7PL Tel: 01676 522978.**

suitable for golfing and angling enthusiasts. Owners Angela and Marc Fowler started building this site in 1994, before which time it was just derelict woodland. By 1996 the site was opened amidst five acres of magnificent woodlands. This peaceful countryside setting is still very convenient for nearby cities and the popular Birmingham NEC, and only half a mile from the village centre, where there is a shop selling provisions and open daily until early evening.

ALLESLEY VILLAGE
10 miles SE of Birmingham off the A45

MAP 4 REF E4

This attractive village midway between Birmingham and Coventry is set amidst picturesque countryside.

The Rainbow Inn and Brewery occupies an early 19th century Grade II listed whitewashed brick building overlaying the original timber-framed structure, which dates back to the 1600s. Brimming with traditional charm, it boasts floor-to-ceiling beams and a separate, cosy dining area with its own bar. Lunches are available Monday to Saturday and dinners (with full waiter service) Tuesday to Friday. There is a large and pleasant patio area/ beer garden to the rear. Owners Terry and Lyn Rotheram make all visitors feel welcome, and provide a high standard of service and quality. In what were once the old stables, Terry has created a micro brewery and now

Rainbow Inn and Brewery, 73 Birmingham Road, Allesley Village Warwickshire CV5 9GT Tel: 01203 402888 Fax: 01203 407415 email: lynn@rotheram.freeserv.co.uk

regularly brews two bitters: Piddlebrook 3.8 strength, named after the village brook, and Firecracker 4.8 strength, which takes its name from the fact that it was first brewed one Bonfire night. Visitors are welcome to make an accompanied tour of the micro brewery. The menu offers a good and varied choice of dishes, all home-prepared and home-cooked, and making use of fresh local ingredients where available.

BOURNVILLE   MAP 1 REF B4
4 miles S of Birmingham off the A4040

This planned village built by the Cadbury family, which moved its factory from the city centre in 1879, is a testament to good labour relations. **Cadbury World** is located in the heart of the famous Bournville factory. Here visitors can follow the story of chocolate, from tropical rainforests to 16th century Spain and on to Georgian London and, finally, Victorian Birmingham. Of course, a highlight of any tour here is the chance to sample the modern day product!

In the heart of Cadbury Village, **Selly Manor** comprises two carefully restored and maintained timber-framed Tudor houses, furnished in keeping with the period and surrounded by abundant gardens. Chocolate magnate George Cadbury saved the Manor from demolition in the late 1800s; his son Lawrence carried on the restoration work by combing Europe in search of accurate furnishings, some of which date back to 1500.

COVENTRY

Although on the fringe of the West Midlands conurbation, Coventry is surrounded by some of the finest scenery and places of historic interest in the country. It claims among many of its famous native sons and daughters the novelist George Eliot, who attended boarding school in Warwick Row and lived with her father here between 1841 and 1849 in Floeshill Road, and poet Philip Larkin, born in the city in 1922.

The three spires of Coventry's **Christchurch, Holy Trinity** and **St Michael's** dominate the city skyline. During the terrible bombing inflicted on the city during the Second World War, St Michael's suffered direct hits. Its spire and ruined windows are all that remains, evoking both the horror and the spirit of reconciliation that arose from those times. Standing in the ruins of these 14th century remains can be a strange and moving experience. The altar is made of broken stones gathered from the night of 15th November 1940. It is surmounted by a cross of charred roof beams and a cross of medieval nails, behind which are inscribed the words from Calvary, 'Father Forgive.'

The new **Cathedral**, designed by Basil Spence, stands by its side, and together they symbolise sacrifice and resurrection. Yet unashamedly modern, its vast and striking interior conveys a powerful sense of the past. It is not only in the two cathedrals that Coventry has shown its indomitable spirit. It is hard to imagine that in the space of one night in November the city centre was gutted, 46,000 homes severely damaged and nearly 75 per cent of the industrial area was almost destroyed. The Cathedral Visitor Centre, in the Undercroft, tells the story of the historical events which took place in Coventry, including the Blitz and its aftermath and the cathedral's role in reconciliation worldwide through the Community of the Cross of Nails.

The city's most famous legend, of course , is that of Lady Godiva, who rode the streets naked to protest against taxation on the 11th century town-dwellers. A bronze statue in Broadgate stands in her memory. It was Leofric who started commerce and industry in Coventry as early as 1043, when he chose the small Saxon township as the site for a Benedictine monastery. He gave the monks land on which to raise sheep, laying the basis for the wool trade which made Coventry prosperous for over 500 years. The story has it, though, that this hard-hearted man taxed the people too heavily and Godiva begged him to lessen the burden. She apparently took the advance precaution of sending her messengers to request everyone stay indoors behind closed shutters before she rode out. One 'Peeping Tom' disregarded her request and was struck blind. The Earl, duly chastened, relented and the taxes were cut.

This modern city has many ancient treasures: **Bond's Hospital** in Hill Street is a beautiful 16th century Tudor almshouse, now a home for the elderly. The exterior and courtyard are open to the public. **Ford's Hospital** in Greyfriar's Lane is another half-timbered Tudor almshouse founded in 1509 by Coventry merchant William Ford. Repaired after the Second World War, it is still used as an almshouse for elderly women, and is considered one of the finest examples of vernacular domestic architecture. Exterior only viewable to the public.

Another half-timbered building, **Cheylesmore Manor House** in New Union Street, was once owned by the Black Prince when he was Lord of the Manor. This attractive half-timbered building is now used as the Register Office, and as such is the oldest in Britain, dating back to 1250. Nearby, in Whitefriars Gate, is the **Toy Museum**, which houses a collection dating from the 18th century. In London Road stands **Whitefriars**, a renovated Carmelite friary dating from 1342 which plays host to art exhibitions, theatre productions and concerts. Near the cathedral is the **Herbert Art Gallery and Museum**, which includes the story of Coventry and reconstructed rooms showing weaving and other skills that have been associated with the city over the years.

In Bayley Lane is **St Mary's Guildhall**, where Kings and Queens have been entertained and Mayors appointed to their office since the 14th century. Its tower once imprisoned Mary, Queen of Scots, and it has a restored 600 year-old crypt. This medieval treasure showcases the city's earliest industrial prosperity, which was founded on wool and cloth. The Guildhall also contains a splendour of old glass, a wealth of carving and a delightful minstrel's gallery with the additional bonus of a unique tapestry. This is one of England's finest Guildhalls, dating back to 1342. Here we see the Arras tapestry, the breathtaking Great North Window, the oak ceiling, and many suits of medieval armour.

The traditional industries of the city - clock-making and silk-weaving - came under threat from Switzerland and France respectively, and during the rapid slump in the city's fortunes many families emigrated to the Americas. It was cycle-making and engineering that ushered in a new wave of prosperity for the city. In 1885, J K Starley invented and produced the modern bicycle. By 1896 Daimler and Humber had opened Coventry's first automotive factories. It was not long before they were joined by other companies, as Coventry became a magnet for labour from all over Britain. In 1930 a Coventrian, Frank Whittle, patented the jet engine. The **Museum of British Road Transport** in St Agnes Lane, Hales Street, examines the enormous contribution made by the city to the transport industry, spanning over 100 years, from the first cycles to the very latest advances in technology. Over 400 magnificent cars, motorcycles, cycles and commercial vehicles are on display.

A few minutes' walk from the city centre, **Coventry Canal Basin** has a distinguished history. It opened to boat traffic in September 1769, and the warehouses on Leicester Row span the late 18th to early 20th centuries. These warehouses, originally built for unloading and storing bulk goods, have been restored and are now home to artists' studios, boat-builders and specialist craft workshops.

Coventry also boasts some outstanding parkland and public spaces. **Lady Herbert's Garden** in Hales Street lies near two of the town's ancient gates. It is a beautiful secluded garden which incorporates part of the old city wall. **Greyfriars Green** in Greyfriars Road is a conservation area with attractive open land and two distinct terraces of fine buildings. The **War Memorial Park** in Kenilworth Road is Coventry's premier park, with beautiful tree-lined walkways, a Peace Garden and Cenotaph.

Coombe Country Park, a few miles east of the city centre off the B4027, comprises almost 400 acres of beautiful historic parkland with formal gardens, woodland and lakeside walks which make up the grounds of Coombe Abbey, landscaped by 'Capability' Brown. It has taken 10 centuries and the vision of many people for this magnificent country park to reach its present splendour. Home to Warwickshire's largest heronry, it also boasts bird hides, picnic area, and informative Visitors' Centre, as well as a restaurant, bar and gift shop.

Just 10 minutes from Coventry city centre, **Vardre** Guest House occupies a turn-of-the-century townhouse. Owners Val and John Smith have lived here for 12 years and have been providing quality bed and breakfast for the last 10 years. The guest house's name comes from a small range of hills in North Wales, Val's home for many years. Open all year round, there are three handsome and very spacious guest bedrooms. Val and John were unwilling to tamper with the rooms' original features, so they are not ensuite. Breakfast in this friendly establishment is a real treat with home-made marmalade one of the specialities. Evening meals are available upon request; vegetarians, vegans and people on special diets are happily catered for. Val and John are very hospitable, and

Vardre, 68 Spencer Avenue, Coventry Warwickshire CV5 6NP Tel: 01203 715154.

knowledgeable about the local area. They take great care in providing a good standard of service, and will make every effort to ensure guests have a relaxing and very comfortable stay.

AROUND COVENTRY

EXHALL   MAP 4 REF E4
3 miles N of Coventry off the A444

Exhall is home to some pretty black-and-white timbered houses; there are also some gentle hill walks in the vicinity.

The Bull & Anchor, part of the Greene King range of public houses, is a pristine whitewashed and very attractive pub located in this handsome village. Very much a hub of village life, the interior of this handsome establishment boasts lots of small alcoves, and is adorned with bygone memorabilia which complements the traditional furnishings and decor.

The Bull & Anchor, Wheelwright Lane, Ash Green, Exhall, Coventry Warwickshire CV7 9HN Tel: 01203 365528.

Licensees Simon and Sally Wilcox took over here in the autumn of 1998, bringing with them over seven years' experience in the trade. They have plenty of enthusiasm for their work and it shows in the care and quality of service they bring to all their guests. Real ales available include Webster's Green Label, Brew XI and John Smith's Smooth, as well of course draught stouts, lagers and cider and bottled beers from around the world. The food draws fans and recommendations from near and far, as the menu mixes old and new to great effect: Specialities include massive steaks, a wonderful chicken, gammon and leek pie, Greek-style pastitsio (a noodle and vegetable dish) and tempting snacks like garlic bread and Cumberland sausage.

BROWNSHILL GREEN   MAP 4 REF E4
3 miles NW of Coventry off the A45

This picturesque Warwickshire hamlet is very close to Coventry city centre yet retains a peaceful rural atmosphere.

The White Lion is a distinguished public house with a long history. First built in the early 1800s, this whitewashed brick home saw life as the village shop and off-licence before being converted into a pub. It took its name from another old village pub which had closed down some years before. Louise Moore has been licensee here since 1976; her father was tenant of the pub before that. The decor is very attractive, as the pub has been renovated and refurbished to its former grandeur, with lots of ex-

The White Lion, Hawkesmill Lane, Brownshill Green, Coventry Warwickshire CV5 9FQ Tel: 01203 332841.

posed hardwoods, half- and full-panelled walls, leaded windows and old prints and memorabilia, including antique farming tools, adorning the walls. There is also a large and very pleasant beer garden. The menu boasts a comprehensive range of bar snacks, light lunches and main courses, as well as daily specials. The excellent ales available include Bass and Brew XI. Throughout there is a warm atmosphere, and all visitors are given a friendly welcome. Open all day seven days a week; last food orders 9.30 p.m.

BAGINTON   MAP 4 REF E5
5 miles S of Coventry off the A444

The Midland Air Museum at Coventry Airport in Baginton houses a unique collection of aircraft, engines and exhibits telling the story of the jet engine. In this hands-on museum visitors can sit in the cockpit of a Vulcan Bomber or Meteor, and with over 35 aircraft on display there is something to interest everyone. This very relaxed and informal museum features local aviation history, with a 'Wings Over Coventry' gallery and a wealth of Coventry-produced aircraft and other exhibits, dominated by the giant Armstrong Whitworth Argosy freighter of 1959. The museum guides are happy to offer information and make all visitors feel welcome.

The museum shop sells model kits, painting and prints of aircraft; there's also a cosy tea room. Open: April-October Monday-Saturday 10 a.m.-5

**The Midland Air Museum, Coventry Airport, Baginton
Warwickshire CV8 3AZ Tel/Fax: 01203 301033.**

p.m., Sundays and Bank Holidays 10 a.m.-6 p.m.; November-March every day 10 a.m.-4.30 p.m. At other times by prior arrangement. Closed Christmas and Boxing Day.

STONELEIGH   MAP 4 REF E5
6 miles S of Coventry off the A444

This attractive village has a sandstone Norman church, several timber-framed houses and, nearby, the headquarters of the Royal Agricultural Society of England, and the Showground famed for its annual Royal Show.

BUBBENHALL   MAP 4 REF F5
7 miles SE of Coventry off the A445

Between Bubbenhall and Ryton-on-Dunsmore, off the A445, **Ryton Pools Country Park** is a new 100 acre country park with an exciting range of facilities, including a Visitors' Centre, picnic areas, bird hide, numerous footpaths, model railway, fishing site and two adventure playgrounds.

Situated in the picturesque hamlet of Bubbenhall, very near the Showground, the traditional public house **The Three Horseshoes** is distinguished in appearance both inside and out. Kim and John Holloway have been here since 1987, and have worked hard to maintain the pub's charm and character. They have built up a reputation for a high standard of service and hospitality. The inn is popular locally and further afield for its excellent food, ale and atmosphere.

Food is available lunchtimes and evenings Monday-Friday and all day at weekends. The menu is outstanding and varied, to suit all tastes. To

**The Three Horseshoes, Springhill, Bubbenhall, Coventry
Warwickshire CV8 3BD Tel: 01203 302108.**

complement this fine selection of snacks and meals there are real ales including Bass and Brew XI as well as a range of lagers, ciders, wines and
spirits. The decor boasts exposed beams and a wealth of bygone memorabilia on display. Open Monday-Thursday 11 a.m.-2.30 p.m. and 5-11 p.m.;
Friday 11 a.m.-3 p.m. and 5-11 p.m.; Saturday 11-11 and Sunday noon-
10.30.

2 Rugby and Eastern Warwickshire

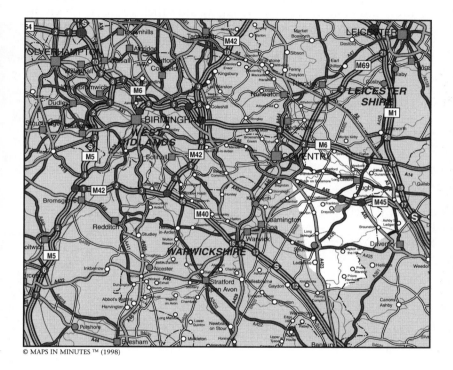

© MAPS IN MINUTES ™ (1998)

Rugby, home of the famous public school which introduced the game of rugby football to the world, is the largest town by far in this region of Warwickshire, which is predominated by smaller and very picturesque villages and hamlets. This part of the county is also home to some outstanding country parks, woodland and waterways.

The Oxford and Union Canals run through it, as do the Rivers Leam, Avon, Itchen and Swift, all affording a wealth of boating and watersports facilities as well as some very peaceful and attractive walks along the towpath and riverbanks. This part of the county is also rich in its own history, having seen the hatching and foiling of the Gunpowder Plot in 1605, and some of the greatest battles of the English Civil War. The region also boasts many fine museums.

RUGBY

The only town of any great size in northeastern Warwickshire, Rugby's Market Place is surrounded by handsome buildings which act as reminders of the town's origins during the reign of Henry III. The **Church of St Andrew** was built by the Rokeby family after their castle had been destroyed by Henry II. The old tower dates from the 1400s. With its fireplace and 3 foot-thick walls, it looks more like a fortress and was, indeed, a place of refuge. The nave and second tower were the work of William Butterfield.

Rugby, however, is probably most famous for **Rugby School**, founded in 1567. Having originally been situated near the Clock Tower in the town, it moved to its present site in 1750. Their are many fine buildings, splendid examples of their period, the highlight being the school chapel, designed by William Butterfield. These buildings house treasures such as stained

Rugby School

glass believed to be the work of Albrecht Durer, the 15th century German artist and engraver.

There are few places in the world where you can gaze with any certainty over the birthplace of a sport that gives pleasure to millions. The game of Rugby originated here at the school when William Webb Ellis broke the rules during a football match in 1823 by picking up and running with the ball.

The school has not always been the calm and peaceful seat of learning that it is today. In November 1797, the Riot Act was read to a group of rebellious pupils, who had made a bonfire of books, pictures and other school property before retreating to the moated island in the school grounds. They were eventually captured by a large force of soldiers, schoolmasters and volunteers from the town, who waded through the water to the island.

Brookes restaurant and coffee house on Bank Street in Rugby has built up an excellent reputation for good food, drink and service. Set in a handsome road among a diversity of interesting local shops in the town centre, just 5 minutes from the famous Rugby School, it is a popular meeting place for townsfolk and visitors alike. The interior is spacious, bright and inviting, with handsome pine furnishings and comfortable seating. The friendly staff offer an excellent choice of fresh coffees and tea and an extensive range of meals, from morning coffee and afternoon tea (the home-made scones and cakes should not be missed) to full lunch or dinner, with wines, beer or spirits from the licensed bar. This charming

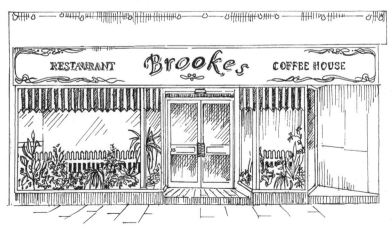

**Brookes, 15 Bank Street, Rugby, Warwickshire CV21 2QE
Tel: 01788 552202.**

establishment takes its name from the poet Rupert Brooke (1887-1915), a native son of Rugby who penned the famous lines;

'If I should die, think only this of me
That there's some corner of a foreign field
That is forever England'

shortly before his death during the First World War. Open 9.15 - 5 p.m. Monday to Saturday.

Rugby School Museum is an award-winner, featuring displays and exhibits highlighted with sound and music which bring to life the school's history, its place in the history of rugby football and the lives of its more notable pupils, such as the poets Matthew Arnold and Rupert Brooke, and mathematician and writer Charles Lutwidge Dodgson (Lewis Carroll), and Thomas Hughes, whose Tom Brown's Schooldays was based on his life at Rugby. Visitors will learn a great deal about the remarkable events in a history dating back to 1567. Guided tours leave from the School Museum Tuesday-Saturday 2.30 throughout the year, except over the Christmas period.

Built in 1851 in Victorian Gothic style, **4 Arnold Villas** is a listed building of great charm and character. This wonderful retreat occupies a quiet, secluded position close to the town centre and within the leafy and peaceful Rugby School Conservation Area. There are four very comfortable guest bedrooms with high ceilings and lovely furnishings. The family collection of period furniture adds to the cosiness and comfort; the guests' lounge and dining room are embellished with a wealth of local memorabilia, prints and maps. On fine days guests can enjoy their full English breakfast in the small Mediterranean garden surrounded by exotics and mature palms. Proprietor

4 Arnold Villas, Rugby, Warwickshire
CV21 3AX Tel: 01788 562626.

Patrick Pratt makes every effort to ensure that guests have an enjoyable and relaxing stay.

Here in the heart of Rugby, in Castle Street, a pedestrianised area, **The Mixed Spice Coffee Lounge** is a cosy, comfortable and charming cafe/ restaurant. Owner Margaret Gill has been here since July of 1998, and is ably assisted by Tina, her partner in an outdoor catering service, and by Mandy, their hard-working assistant. The building dates back to the late 1900s, and is a good example of simple yet impressive redbrick Victorian

**Mixed Spice Coffee Lounge, 13a Castle Street, Rugby
Warwickshire CV21 2TP Tel: 01788 562509.**

architecture. The range of food available, most of it home-made, is varied, offering a selection of hot and cold snacks and meals, including the daily Roast of the Day, a popular favourite. All the selections are hearty and filling, from the fresh scones and cakes to the soups and salads. Fresh local ingredients are used wherever possible. All can be washed down with one of a fine range of teas, coffees and soft drinks. Open Monday/Friday/Saturday 8 a.m.-4 p.m., Tuesday-Thursday 8 a.m.-3.30 p.m.

Rugby Town Trail is a two-hour walk that brings to life the history of this attractive market town from its Saxon beginnings to the present day. The walk begins and ends at the Clock Tower in Market Place. This edifice was intended to commemorate the Golden Jubilee of Queen Victoria in 1887, yet it was not completed until 1889 because over-indulgent citizens had dipped too deep into the Tower funds to feast and drink at the Jubilee. You will see many of the town's main tourist attractions, including the house where Rupert Brooke was born, and his statue in Regent Place. Information and maps of the trail are available from Rugby Library, the Town Hall or the town's museums.

For shoppers, there is a good selection of specialist shops at Clock Towers, North Street, Rugby's premier indoor shopping centre. Churchside Arcade is a small complex of craft, fashion and gift shops in Little Church Street. Rugby Market holds traditional markets every Monday, Friday and Saturday.

Rugby is also the home of the **James Gilbert Rugby Museum**, housed in the original building where, since 1842, the Gilberts have been making their world-famous rugby footballs. This Museum is crammed with memorabilia of the game and its development.

Rugby Football Museum

Summersault is an attractive and welcoming Egon Ronay-recommended coffee house/restaurant and shop in Rugby's pedestrianised High Street. Occupying a distinctive 19th century building near to Rugby School, this cosy shop has a brasserie atmosphere, enhanced by the hanging baskets, trails of flowers and climbing plants all round the exterior (the shop has won the 'Blooming Rugby' award five years in a row). The aroma of coffee beans, loose teas and freshly baked quiches, scones, cakes, pizzas

**Summersault, 27 High Street, Rugby, Warwickshire CV21 3BW
Tel: 01788 543223.**

and bread rolls draws customers in to sample the delights on offer, which also include 12 varieties of salads, 10 choices of sweets and puddings and 20 different types of coffees and teas. Lunch is served from about 11 a.m. There is also a tasteful selection of objets d'art, craftware, jewellery and women's clothing for sale, making this an excellent place to eat and to shop for that unusual and exceptional gift. Open: restaurant 9-4.30; shop 9-5.30. Closed Sundays.

Caldecott Park in the centre of town has beautiful floral displays, trees and a herb garden. Picnicking areas and a play area are two more of the highlights of this lovely park, and there are also facilities for bowls, putting, tennis and boules.

Rugby is bounded by two of the greatest Roman roads, Fosse Way and Watling Street, which meet just northwest of Rugby, at High Cross. This is one of the landmarks of the area.

The town is as far inland as it is possible to get in the British Isles, yet Rugby is an excellent centre for all kinds of water sports and aquatic activities. The Oxford Canal winds its way through the borough, and the Rivers Avon, Leam and Swift provide good angling, pleasant walks and places to picnic.

Cock Robin Wood is a nature reserve on Dunchurch Road, near the junction with Ashlawn Road. Here the visitor will find extensive areas of oak, ash, rowan, cherry and field maples, as well as grassy areas and a central pond, a haven for insects, frogs and butterflies.

The **Great Central Walk** is a four-mile ramble through Rugby. Along the way visitors will encounter an abundance of wildlife, plants and shrubs, as well as conservation areas and picnic sites.

AROUND RUGBY

DUNCHURCH   MAP 4 REF G5
1½ miles S of Rugby off the A426

'The gunpowder plot village': on November 5th, 1605, the Gunpowder Plot conspirators met at the Red Lion Inn, Dunchurch, to await the news

Dunchurch Village

of Guy Fawkes' success in blowing up the English Houses of Parliament. The Red Lion still exists today, as a private residence known as **Guy Fawkes House**. This attractive village with its rows of thatched cottages has a 14th-century church built by the monks of Pipewell Abbey, with one of the oldest parish registers in England.

The earliest mention of this historic and picturesque village, however, is some 500-plus years before the Gunpowder Plot, in the Domesday Book of 1086, where it appears as *Donecerce*. With a population of only 130 at the time, it was the property of William of Osbourne, the son of a Norman noble, who had claimed it during the Norman Conquest.

Situated within the square of this historic village, a village at one time much larger than Rugby itself, **Little L's Fabrics**, The Patchwork Place, is a mine of information and materials for patchwork, quilting and other craft projects. Owner Laura Cox has a wealth of experience in patchwork and quilting, and is happy to help with any questions her customers might have about what to choose from the vast range of patchwork, quilting and embroidery materials and accessories on hand. Throughout the year the shop also hosts day workshops and evening and day classes covering, for example, stenciling, sewing, making handmade

Little L's Fabrics, 6 The Square, Dunchurch, Warwickshire CV22 6NU Tel: 01788 810959.

Christmas decorations, and much more. Open Tuesday and Thursday-Saturday 10 a.m.-5 p.m., Wednesday 10 a.m.-1 p.m., and Sunday 12-4 p.m. Closed Mondays.

Such was the considerable trade in looking after travellers who stopped over in Dunchurch during the great coaching days (up to 40 coaches a day stopped here), it is said that every property in the centre of the village was at some time an inn or ale house. For centuries Dunchurch has been a popular stopover point for travellers on the main Holyhead-London road. A coaching stop to take on fresh horses, Dunchurch was also the staging post for pupils, masters, parents and visitors travelling to Rugby School. Many famous and important people have stayed in the village over the centuries, including Princess Victoria, Longfellow, the Duke of Wellington and William Webb Ellis of Rugby Football fame. Today, the village is in a designated conservation area with a lovely village green complete with village stocks and maypole, charming 16th, 17th and 18th century buildings, many of which retain the traditional Warwickshire thatched roofs. In 1996 the village won the prestigious *Best Kept Large Village in Warwickshire* award.

The **Village Green Hotel** in Dunchurch is a lovely and supremely comfortable establishment located in the heart of this picturesque and tranquil village. There are 10 spacious rooms in all, four on the ground floor, six on the first, all ensuite and all superbly appointed and furnished. One has a four-poster bed, for that extra bit of luxury. Each room has been given the name of a famous person, from the Princess Victoria and Earl of Warwick to the Dick Turpin and William Webb Ellis (inventor of Rugby football). Owned by business partners Tony Kember and Paula Twigger since January 1997, it underwent a £100,000 refurbishment and re-opened in May of that year, and now enjoys an ever-growing popularity and reputation for its high standard of service and comfort. With facilities for the

**The Village Green Hotel, The Green, Dunchurch, Rugby
Warwickshire CV22 6NX Tel: 01788 813434 Fax: 01788 814714
email: villagegreenhotel.rugby@btinternet.com**

business person and tourer alike, every possible need has been thought of in this elegant hotel. English Tourist Board Highly Commended.

Every year the village is host to the **Dunchurch Festival of Fire**, on the Saturday nearest to the 5th November.

Foxgloves Gardens at 35 Rugby Road in Dunchurch are small gardens with an ornamental potager, fruit cage, cordon fruit trees, grapes, figs, kiwi fruit, herb garden, lawn with colour-themed herbaceous borders, ornamental shrubs, climbing roses and collections of foxgloves and hardy geraniums. Other village gardens are also sometimes open to the public. Please phone 01788 817643 for details.

The Old Smithy which stands on the Rugby Road, is believed to have been the inspiration for Henry Wadsworth Longfellow's poem *'Under the Spreading Chestnut Tree'*.

DRAYCOTE   Map 4 ref F5
4 miles SW of Rugby off the A426

Draycote Water is a centre of watersports, fishing, sailing, birdwatching and attractive walks around the reservoir. Fly fishing permits are available from the Fishing Lodge. **Draycote Country Park**, next to Draycote Water, boasts 21 acres for walks, kite flying, picnicking by the lake, and magnificent hilltop views over Draycote Water, one of the largest reservoirs in the region.

MARTON   Map 4 ref F5
5 miles SW of Rugby off the A423

Marton village is home to the **Museum of Country Bygones**, a cornucopia of rural and agricultural memorabilia dating from the 19th century.

PRINCETHORPE   Map 4 ref F5
6 miles NE of Leamington Spa off the B4453

Paxford in Princethorpe is a flower-arranger's garden, part of the National Gardens Scheme Charitable Trust (telephone 01926 624304 for details). Featuring heathers and fuchsias, the garden has been designed and maintained by the owners as a series of rooms.

Set in the midst of beautiful Warwickshire countryside, with outstanding views of the surrounding gardens and grounds, **The Woodhouse** is a distinguished and attractive restaurant and hotel. Once a farmhouse, it was converted into an hotel long before owners Julia and Desmond Grundy purchased it over 30 years ago. The oldest part of this gracious building, the old barn, now converted and refurbished, dates back to the 1600s. The cuisine on offer at this elegant establishment is of the highest quality,

Woodhouse Hotel & Restaurant, Leamington Road, Princethorpe
Warwickshire CV23 9PZ Tel/Fax: 01926 632131/632303.

whether guests make their selection from the bar menu, Carvery or the à la carte menu. Specialities from the tempting menu include fresh salmon, chicken breast with wild mushrooms and grilled sirloin steak, all prepared and presented with great style. Open lunchtimes and evenings every day. Booking is advised. The restaurant's elegant interior, quality cuisine and high standard of service ensure a unique dining experience. The hotel boasts 17 beautifully appointed ensuite letting rooms. Seven are situated in the main building, 10 in an adjacent annex. All are furnished and decorated to a high standard of style, comfort and taste. The hospitality on offer is top of the range; guests are assured a warm and genuine welcome, and its location makes it an ideal base from which to explore this beautiful part of the county.

FRANKTON   MAP 4 REF F5
5 miles SW of Rugby off the A423/A45

This very rustic and picturesque village boasts some handsome and historic cottages. **The Friendly Inn** here in Frankton lives up to its name with a growing reputation for genuine warmth and hospitality. Originally the home of Richard Fosterd, founder of Fosterd's Bridge Charity in the mid-16th century, the property was rented out after his death, to raise money for the charity to be used in building and maintaining many of the local bridges and roads. By 1903 the property had become a public house. Well recommended for its good food, ale and atmosphere, the menu boasts a range of tempting meals including traditional favourites such as haddock and chips, ham, egg and chips, and curry dishes. All are home-made

**The Friendly Inn, Main Street, Frankton, Nr Rugby
Warwickshire CV23 9NY Tel: 01926 632430.**

and make use of fresh local produce wherever possible. There are also very good daily specials. The real ales available are ever-changing; some come from local breweries. Proprietor Nick Rushbrooke has owned the pub since 1997; he and his amiable staff maintain the pub's success and reputation for a high quality of service.

LONG ITCHINGTON   Map 4 ref F6
8 miles SW of Rugby off the A423

The picturesque village of Long Itchington straddles the lovely Grand Union Canal. The Anglo-Saxon *'Farm by the River Itchen'* boasted a population greater than that of Coventry at the time of the Domesday Book. The village Church of the Holy Trinity dates in part from 1190. The tower has only the remains of its original spire, which collapsed when struck by lightning during a Sunday morning service in 1762. The carvings in the chancel bear a closer look: one depicts a monkey with her young, another the head and shoulders of what is believed to be a jester.

The Cuttle Inn stands alongside the Grand Union Canal in Long Itchington, just a mile or so north of Southam. It takes its unusual name from Anglo-Saxon times, when a cuttle was a man-made channel leading to a watermill. Owners Roger and Julie bought the inn in 1993. It had stood derelict for two years when they purchased it; their hard work and goodwill have now transformed it into a characterful, cosy and charming country inn with an excellent range of real ales and a genuine air of hospitality and warmth.

Bed and breakfast accommodation is available here as well, in the two large twins and one single room. The adjacent **Five Oaks Canalside Restaurant** offers a superb menu featuring hearty traditional favourites, all served with great style. Specialities include the homemade steak and mush-

Cuttle Inn & Five Oaks Restaurant, Southam Road, Long Itchington Nr Rugby, Warwickshire CV23 8QZ Tel: 01926 812314/811022.

room pie and the mixed grill. Both establishments offer guests a truly relaxing and enjoyable experience.

SOUTHAM   Map 4 ref F6
9 miles SW of Rugby off the A426

Southam is an attractive town along the River Itchen. It repays a visit for the lovely rural scenery surrounding the town, and the wealth of good walking in the area. It was here in Southam that Charles I spend the night before the battle of Edgehill. The Roundheads also came into the town, and Cromwell himself arrived with 7,000 troops in 1645. In the main street is the surprisingly named **Old Mint Inn**, a 14th century stone building taking its name from an occurrence following the Battle of Edgehill. Charles I commanded his local noblemen to bring him their silver treasure, which was then melted down and minted into coins with which he paid his army.

Just half a mile east of Southam town centre and set in rural surroundings, **Tarsus Hotel & Restaurant** is a convivial and very pleasant family-run

Tarsus Hotel & Restaurant, Daventry Road, Southam Warwickshire CV33 0NW Tel: 01926 813585.

establishment specialising in Greek and Turkish dishes. The full a la carte menu includes good selection of fish and vegetarian meals. On the first Monday of each month, the house speciality, Meze, which incorporates 20 different dishes in one meal, is served. The Mediterranean flavour of the restaurant is enhanced by the attractive murals of Cyprus. The full licensed bar has a good selection of malt whiskies and a fine wine list. Diners can enjoy their meal either in the restaurant itself or outdoors in the attractive courtyard, which bridges the area between the restaurant and the guest bedrooms. There are 12 ensuite rooms, many overlooking the attractive gardens. Two of these are luxury suites: The Aphrodite features a four-poster bed and Jacuzzi bath, while the Jasmine has a lovely brass bedstead and Jacuzzi bath. Open 7 days.

RYTON-ON-DUNSMORE

MAP 4 REF F5

6 miles W of Rugby off the A45

This village is home to the Henry Doubleday Research Association at **Ryton Gardens**. This organic farming and gardening organisation leads the way in research and advances in horticulture. The grounds are landscaped with thousands of plants and trees, all organically grown. There is also on site a herb garden, rose garden, garden for the blind, shrub borders and free-range animals. Special events are held throughout the year.

Ryton Pools Country Park is a 100 acre country park opened in 1996. The 10 acre Ryton Pool is home to Greatcrested Grebes, Swans, Moorhen and Canada Geese. There is also an attractive meadow area for strolling or picnicking, Visitor Centre, shop and exhibition area. Pagets Pool near the northeastern end of the park is one of the most important sites in Warwickshire for dragonflies, with 17 species including the Common Blue, Emperor Dragonfly and Black-tailed Skimmer. Other highlights include guided walks and a model railway run by Coventry Model Engineering Society.

LONG LAWFORD

MAP 4 REF G4

1½ W of Rugby off the A428

Long Lawford is a beautiful village along the banks of the River Avon. Just a mile and a half from Rugby centre, **Lodge Farm** in Long Lawford is a camping and caravan site occupying a five-acre smallholding. Owned and run by Alec and Jane Brown, and set in lovely countryside, this excellent site has facilities for up to 35 campers, caravans or tents. Featuring soft standings on level grass, all with electric hook-ups, there is also a brand new toilet and showers block. Also on-site are two lovely self-catering cottages, barn conversions of the highest order, with full facilities and ideal to use as a base for exploring this lovely part of the county. Each cottage

**Lodge Farm, Bilton Lane, Long Lawford, Rugby
Warwickshire CV23 9DU Tel: 01788 560193.**

sleeps two, and is equipped with every modern convenience. Half a mile
further on from the farm, Alec and Jane also provide bed and breakfast
accommodation in a lovely and comfortable house with five double rooms.
Whatever your choice of accommodation, Lodge Farm can provide it. Camp
site open Easter-end October. Self-catering cottages and B&B available all
year round.

BRETFORD   MAP 4 REF F4
5 miles SE of Coventry off the B4029

This lovely village on the River Avon has a name which means 'ford of the
Britons', as the Fosse Way crosses the river here.

Queens Head is an attractive and extensive roadside public house and
restaurant. This family-run establishment has a welcoming atmosphere
and is popular with locals and visitors alike. A 19th century former coaching inn featuring the original ceiling beams, it has been tastefully enlarged
by the addition of three adjacent cottages. There is a large, relaxing garden
which includes a children's playground area. The menu offers much more
than standard fare: a large selection of fish meals, steaks, and other traditional English favourites is augmented in the evening menu by sumptuous
surprises for the intrepid guest: ostrich, wild boar, kangaroo and barracuda
are among the specialities. The home-made pies are also a real treat, as are
the traditional English puddings. The wine list offers an excellent choice.

Local historical sites include neolithic and early Bronze Age enclosures,
Roman baths from a natural spring and a Roman pathway to nearby
Brinklow.

**Queens Head, Bretford, Nr Coventry, Warwickshire CV23 0JY
Tel: 01203 542671.**

BRANDON   MAP 4 REF F4
5 miles W of Rugby off the A428

Brandon Marsh Nature Centre is 200 acres of lakes, marshes, woodland
and grassland, providing a home and haven for many species of wildlife.
There are bird hides, an informative Visitors' Centre and a Nature Trail, as
well as guided walks, pond-dipping and changing exhibitions.

Brandon Wood Municipal Golf Club is an 18-hole, 6,600 yard, par 72
course with floodlit driving range, restaurant and bar, open to non-mem-
bers.

STRETTON-UNDER-FOSSE   MAP 4 REF F4
5 miles NW of Rugby off the B4112

For a slightly unusual day out, **H M Prison Services Museum** at Newbold
Revel, Stretton-under-Fosse has displays on the history of imprisonment
from medieval times to the present. Visits are strictly by appointment;
contact the Curator on 01788 834168.

NEWBOLD-ON-AVON   MAP 4 REF G4
1 mile N of Rugby off the B4112

Newbold Quarry Park affords visitors the opportunity for a country walk just north of Rugby town, with hilly woodland and extensive waterside walks. This bit of countryside is a haven for birds and wildlife.

The epitome of a traditional English inn, **The Barley Mow** stands near the Oxford Canal and the River Avon here in the handsome village of Newbold-on-Avon. A former canal house and barn, it has been the leasehold of Mick Smith for the past 17 years; early in 1998 he handed over the running of the place to his daughter Kerry. During Mick's time here he has transformed the premises into an inn of real quality, with excellent food, ales and a wonderful ambience. Among the ales on offer are Stones, Tetleys,

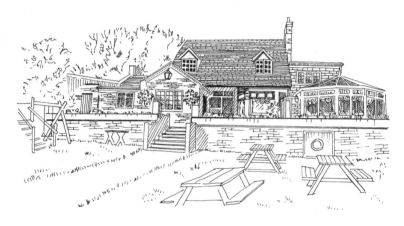

The Barley Mow, Newbold-on-Avon, Rugby
Warwickshire CV21 1HW Tel: 01788 544174.

Brew XI and Bass, plus guest ales and draught lagers. The menu is varied and impressive, with a special Sunday lunch and many daily specials to add to your options. There are also nine ensuite guest rooms available, should you wish to extend your stay in this very pretty and tranquil part of the county. Brimming with character and charm, guests are certain to enjoy the warm hospitality and high standard of service available.

CLIFTON-UPON-DUNSMORE   Map 4 ref G4
1 mile NE of Rugby off the A5

This very pretty village is home to Clifton Cruisers, which hire out canal boats for holidays and short excursions. **The Bull Inn** here in this picturesque village is a former farmhouse built in 1598 and converted to a public house in the early 1800s. Tom and Dolores Rowan have been the licensees since 1997, bringing with them a wealth of experience in the trade. This characterful, charming pub is tastefully decorated and comfortably furnished throughout, with lots of style. The menu is extensive, and enhanced

**The Bull Inn, 33 Main Street, Clifton-upon-Dunsmore, Nr Rugby
Warwickshire CV23 0BH Tel: 01785 544565.**

with a wonderful array of delicious daily specials (at least 18 special main courses a day). Most of the food is home-made, and makes use of fresh local ingredients wherever possible. Lunch is available from 12-2.30 p.m., dinners from 6.30-9 p.m. every day. Hand in hand with the good food there is a range of real ales, including Ansells, Tetleys, Calders Bitters, and a changing guest ale. Also on tap are draught lagers, ciders, and Guinness. For a truly enjoyable meal and drink, look no further.

KILSBY   MAP 4 REF H5
3 miles SE of Rugby off the A361

This village on the Warwickshire-Northamptonshire border is lovely, with a wealth of attractive walks in the village environs. **The Halfway House** is

**The Halfway House, 1 Watling Street, Kilsby, Nr Rugby
Warwickshire CV23 8YE Tel: 01788 822888.**

an impressive and welcoming hotel and public house occupying an enviable position just 500 yards from junction 18 of the M1 motorway, on the border of Warwickshire and Northamptonshire, near the A5 and M6. This 19th century former coaching inn features six very comfortable ensuite rooms, a well-stocked bar, beer garden and children's playground. There is a good selection of beers and wines, and an extensive menu featuring sumptuous home-cooked meals (the traditional Sunday lunch is a speciality), as well as bar snacks and a special children's menu. Furnished with traditional fittings and adorned with charming paintings, there is an attractive conservatory and separate dining area. This wonderful establishment makes an ideal base for exploring the region, offering guests a warm welcome and home comforts in relaxing surroundings.

ASHBY ST LEDGERS   MAP 4 REF H5
4 miles SE of Rugby off the A361

The Gunpowder Plot conspirators took refuge here in the manor house owned by Robert Catesby. Though not open to visitors, the manor house is close to the road and worth seeing, as it is very evocative of the times. This charming village also rewards a stroll, with some cottages designed by Edward Lutyens. Parts of the handsome village church date back to the early 1500s.

BRAUNSTON   MAP 4 REF G5
5 miles SE of Rugby off the A45

Braunston Marina is a major canal boat centre on the Grand Union Canal. **Braunston Stop House** adjacent to the Marina occupies a former toll house on the canal, and features changing exhibitions throughout the year on the social and cultural life of the waterways.

PRIORS MARSTON   MAP 4 REF G6
9 miles SE of Rugby off the A425

Priors Marston has attractive old houses around a handsome village green, and unusual blue brick paths. There is a good walk up Marston Hill.

NAPTON ON THE HILL   MAP 4 REF G6
9 miles SE of Rugby off the A425

This attractive village on a rounded hill above a curve in the Oxford Canal - one of the prettiest in this part of the world, with pleasant towpath walks. There are views of seven counties from the hilltop.

PRIORS HARDWICK
MAP 4 REF G6

10 miles SE of Rugby off the A425

Priors Hardwick, near the Northamptonshire border, boasts a network of paths taking you down to the Oxford Canal. One of the best-known and highest-esteemed restaurants in the country is here. **The Butchers Arms Restaurant**, dating back to 1375, resembles a large country house, with its mellowed brick walls and sheer scale. The interior epitomises warmth and comfort. Owners Lino and Augusta Pires, originally from Portugal, have built up this highly successful restaurant, formerly a small and rather rundown country pub, over the years. The menu offers a wide range of tempting dishes, all prepared on the premises using the finest fresh produce from near and far. The wine list is both affordable and extensive,

The Butchers Arms Restaurant, Priors Hardwick, Nr Rugby Warwickshire CV23 8SN Tel: 01327 260504 Fax: 01327 260502.

with over 200 wines on offer. The desserts alone are well worth the visit. The presentation and preparation of all dishes in this silver-service restaurant is superb. The friendly and efficient staff offer a very high standard of service. One area of this quality restaurant is adorned with the autographed photos of over 50 celebrities who have enjoyed the unique ambience and superb food - why not join their ranks?

3 Nuneaton and North East Warwickshire

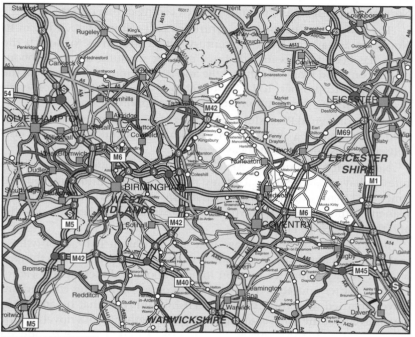

© MAPS IN MINUTES ™ (1998)

Many visitors to Warwickshire overlook this gracious part of the county, to their cost. Here the visitor will find not only some of the prettiest countryside the county has to offer, but also landmarks of the greatest historical and cultural significance. The town of Market Bosworth was the scene of Richard III's defeat to Henry Bolingbroke, thus ushering in the reign of the Tudors, a critical turning point of national importance to the country's religious, industrial and artistic heritage. Some of the significant events surrounding the Civil War were also witnessed by the early inhabitants of this part of Warwickshire. And the region's largest town, Nuneaton, is itself a mine of tradition and history, with a distinctive cultural and industrial legacy all its own. All this in a region that remains in many ways unspoilt in its rural simplicity and pastoral grandeur, with villages that date back to Saxon times and even earlier.

NUNEATON

Originally a Saxon town known at *Etone*, Nuneaton is mentioned in the Domesday Book of 1086. The 'Nun' was added when a wealthy Benedictine priory was founded here in 1290. The **Priory ruins** left standing are adjacent to the church of **St Nicholas**, a Victorian edifice occupying a Norman site which has a beautiful carved ceiling dating back to 1485.

The town has a history as a centre for coal-mining, which began in Nuneaton as early as the 14th century. Other industries for which the town has been famous include brick and tile manufacture and ribbon-making on hand looms. As the textile and hatting industries boomed, the town began to prosper. Today's Nuneaton is a centre of precision engineering, printing, car components and other important trades.

Nuneaton's vivid **Riversley Park** boasts a large recreation area and children's playground, a sports centre and boating facilities as well as lush conservatories and fascinating aviaries.

Nuneaton Museum and Art Gallery, located in Riversley Park, features displays of archaeological interest ranging from prehistoric to medieval times, and items from the local earthenware industry. There is also a permanent exhibition of the town's most illustrious daughter, the novelist and thinker George Eliot.

Born to a prosperous land agent at Arbury Hall in 1819, Eliot (whose real name was Mary Ann Evans) was an intellectual giant and free thinker. She left Warwickshire for London in adulthood, and met George Henry Lewes, a writer and actor who was to become her lifelong companion. Lewes, married with three children, left his family so that he and Eliot, very bravely for the time, could set up house together. Eliot's novels return again and again to the scenes and social conventions of her youth, and are among the greatest works of English - in particular her masterpiece, *Middlemarch*.

A series of walkways extends around the Nuneaton area, linking public footpaths, bridleways, areas of open space, disused railway lines and canal towpaths. This system is known as the **Green Track**. Information and 'Walks Around...' leaflets, available from Nuneaton or Bedworth library and Nuneaton Town Hall and Council House, identify the various routes and points of interest along the way.

Manor Snacks on Manor Court Road in Nuneaton is a smart and welcoming cafe/restaurant offering an extensive selection of freshly cooked meals: breakfasts, morning coffee, crusty bread sandwiches, french sticks and baps, afternoon tea and dinner meals - a full range of tempting snacks available any time of day. Owner David Hatch has many years' experience as a grill chef; after 10 years in charge at the local pub, he started up this delightful cafe early in 1997. He takes great care over the quality and pres-

Manor Snacks, 4A Manor Court Road, Nuneaton
Warwickshire CV11 5HY Tel: 01203 320922.

entation of the delicious meals on offer. As a result, his establishment is popular with both locals and tourists, located as it is just a mile from Nuneaton town centre. Open 7 days a week from 7 a.m. - 7.30 p.m.

The Attleborough Arms is a large, friendly and welcoming public house standing about a mile from the centre of Nuneaton off the B4114. Built as a Davenports house in 1974, it retains a very homely feel inside and out, with a picket fence outside along the quiet, tree-lined street. Latterly a

The Attleborough Arms, Highfield Road, Nuneaton
Warwickshire CV11 4PL Tel: 01203 383231.

Greenalls public house, tenants Darren and Rachel have been here since early in 1998. They are a gregarious, enthusiastic and warm couple, who take pride in making every guest feel comfortable. They and their staff offer a high quality of service which keeps the pub very popular with locals and visitors alike. The pub is tastefully decorated throughout, with an eye towards mixing the best of traditional comforts with every modern convenience. The interior boasts an intriguing portrait of a lady, believed to be the woman whose ghost a number of people - including Darren - have seen. There is also an interesting collection of old bottles on high shelves against one wall, and floor-to-ceiling beams which pass through disused barrels - an evocative decorating touch. The range of ales on offer is very good, including Tetleys, Worthington Smoothflow, Caffrey's and guest ales which change every two to three months. The atmosphere is usually lively and convivial, with a wealth of visitors to this part of Warwickshire taking part in the comforts offered by this outstanding pub.

AROUND NUNEATON

ATTLEBOROUGH   MAP 4 REF F3
1 mile SE of Nuneaton off the B4114

This peaceful and secluded village just outside Nuneaton offers a wealth of attractive walks amid some very pretty countryside. **The Crows Nest** is a welcoming and stylish public house located here on the rural outskirts of Nuneaton. This impressive establishment has recently been completely refurbished - the reclaimed brickwork gives the pub a rural country feel, and this, combined with the comforts and spaciousness of the interior with its open beams to the roofline, plenty of comfortable seating and handsome decor, make for a very attractive and relaxing ambience in which to enjoy a quiet drink and a meal. The decor features agricultural themes - local artists are encouraged to exhibit their work on the walls. There is an

The Crows Nest, Crowhill Road, Attleborough, Nuneaton
Warwickshire CV11 6PJ Tel: 01203 374833.

excellent range of beers, wines and soft drinks, including traditional Banks's Black Country ales. The extensive selection of fresh home-cooked snacks, meals and puddings to tempt visitors' palates; food is served all day, with the lunchtime servery and grills particularly good value. Welcoming and hospitable managers Steve and Melanie Smith bring a fresh approach and are 'genuinely pleased to serve'.

BULKINGTON
MAP 4 REF F3
6 miles NE of Coventry off the B4109

The 13th-century Bulkington Church is mentioned in the Domesday Book, and the village is noted for its weaving, ribbon-making and farming.

Furlongs Farm is a popular and comfortable bed and breakfast. The five attractive and tasteful rooms occupy the former dairy of this farm, having been expertly converted and refurbished to include every modern convenience and comfort. There are ample gardens for relaxing in, and 20 acres of farmland, including an arboretum planted three years ago. The rooms feature country-style fittings, with floral fabrics and attractive pine furnishings. All rooms - two with single bed, three with double beds - are ensuite and have attractive breakfast areas. Guests are served continental breakfast in their rooms, which also feature tea and coffee making facilities. All rooms are non-smoking. There are several good local pubs in the area: The Shilton Arms in Shilton, Rose & Castle in Ansty, and the Royal Oak, Bedworth; and excellent walking in the surrounding countryside.

Furlongs Farm, Shilton Lane, Bulkington, Bedworth Warwickshire CV12 9JP Tel: 01203 313778.

Here in the handsome village of Bulkington, **Clare Abells Tea & Coffee Shop** stands in a quiet spot, a haven of warmth and cosiness. Always a cafe, the building was built 20 years ago. A friendly welcome awaits visitors in need of refreshment. This small establishment is very nicely decorated, and seats 26 comfortably. Owner Jacqueline Smith took over in mid-1998, bringing with her a wealth of experience in catering. Through her culinary talents she has made this charming eatery very popular. The menu features many delicious options, from among traditional favourites such as bacon, sausage and egg platters, toasted sandwiches, burgers, omelettes and salads. Much of it is home-cooked and home-prepared, and the portions are

Clare Abells Tea & Coffee Shop, 6 Leicester Street, Bulkington, Warwickshire CV12 9NG Tel: 01203 640998.

hearty. The waitressing staff are attentive and offer a high standard of service. Open Monday-Saturday 8 a.m.-4 p.m; Sundays in December from 12-2 p.m. There is a special three-course lunch for a set price available Monday-Thursday, with special rates for pensioners.

MONKS KIRBY   MAP 4 REF G4
9 miles SE of Nuneaton off the A427

This very old settlement dates back to about the time of the Bronze Age. Indeed, it is thought that the mound on which the **parish church** now stands was originally built by these primitive people as a meeting place for pagan worship and social gatherings. Following these ancient tribes came the Celts, Romans and Saxons. The Saxons were the first people to build a church on the site, probably a wooden structure originally, being replaced by a stone building later. The Danes arrived about 864 AD as part of their conquest of this part of the country. The field at the rear of the church is still known as the Denmark Field.

After the Norman Conquest, a Benedictine Priory was established and a church rebuilt on the old site. Most of the present building dates from the 14th century. The tall spire, built above the tower in the 15th century, could be seen by travellers for many miles around until it was blown down by a great storm on Christmas night in 1701. From its earliest days Monks Kirby grew in size and importance, eventually taking on the full status of a market town. Pilgrims and merchants were accommodated in the Priory's guest house, which probably stood on the site of the current Denbigh Arms public house. This rural, quiet village, dominated by the ancient church, also boasts many pretty cottages along its main streets.

The impressive **Denbigh Arms** public house dates back to the 17th century. A working farm as well as an inn up to the turn of the last century, it occupies land that was part of the Earl of Denbigh's estate up until 1962. Owners Harry and Susan Morton offer guests a friendly welcome to their handsome rural retreat. The atmosphere is cosy and amiable, with an accent on traditional home comforts. The excellent home-cooked food on offer includes the best in traditional English fare - steaks (including 40-ounce rump roasts!) are a speciality. There is a great selection of malt

Denbigh Arms, Main Street, Monks Kirby, Warwickshire CV23 0QX
Tel: 01788 832303.

whiskies, real ales and popular own-label house wines and ports. Once a month the function room upstairs is host to an award-winning blue grass band. There is additional seating in the front garden when the weather is fine, and a children's play area and collection of animals - including a Vietnamese pig - at the rear. The Mortons also hold the key to the parish church, and are more than happy to show visitors round.

ARBURY HALL   MAP 4 REF E3
3 miles SW of Nuneaton off the B4102

A visit to **Arbury Hall** fits another piece in the jigsaw of George Eliot's life and times. Still the ancestral seat of the Viscount and Viscountess Daventry, and home to the Newdigate family for over 400 years, it is built on the ruins of an Augustinian monastery and is now one of the best examples of 18th century Gothic Revival architecture in the country. Largely the creation of Sir Roger Newdigate, who began the work in 1748, it stands amid rolling lawns and is surrounded by acres of beautiful parkland. This lovely Elizabethan mansion house was refurbished and renovated by Sir Roger during the second half of the 18th century, and boasts soaring fan vaulting, plunging pendants and delicate filigree tracing in most rooms. Before Sir Roger's day, in the 1670s his forebear Sir Richard Newdigate built the impressive stable block - designed partly by Christoper Wren. There are a few works by Christopher Wren in the former stables, which now house a collection of vintage cycles. Arbury contains important collections of paintings, furniture, glass and china collected through the centuies by successive generations of the family.

George Eliot was born on the estate, where her father was land agent; in Mr Gifgil's Love Story she portrays Arbury as Cheverel Manor, and gives detailed descriptions of many of the rooms in the house, including the Saloon and the Dining Room - comparing the latter, unsurprisingly given its grandeur, to a cathedral.

Arbury Hall

The Hall's grounds include a delightful 10 acre garden with a real air of tranquillity about them. The gardens boast bulbs at the start of the season, followed by rhododendrons, azalea and wisteria, then roses from June culminating in autumn colours bursting in the trees and shrubs. Highlights include the formal rose garden, lakes with wildfowl, bluebell woods, pollarded limes and arboretum in the old walled garden.

BEDWORTH   MAP 4 REF F3
4 miles S of Nuneaton off the B4029

This small town was once part of the north Warwickshire coal field established at the end of the 17th century. Local people were largely responsible for the building of the Coventry Canal, running from Coventry to Fradley near Lichfield and completed in 1790, 22 years after work on it began. It was constructed to connect the fast-growing town with the great new trade route, the *Grand Trunk* - and to provide Coventry with cheap coal from the Bedworth coal field.

French Protestant families fleeing persecution sought refuge here, bringing with them their skill in silk and ribbon weaving. The **parish church**, completed in 1890, is a good example of Gothic revival. Outside there is a Scented Garden. The open air market and main shopping precinct share the town's central **All Saints Square** with the splendid **Chamberlain almshouses**, founded in 1663.

Bedworth's award-winning **Miners' Welfare Park** contains some of the finest spring and summer bedding layouts in the region, as well as areas devoted to tennis, bowls, pitch and putt, roller skating and cricket.

ANSLEY   MAP 4 REF E3
5 miles W of Nuneaton off the B4112

Ansley is best known for adjacent **Hoar Park**, which dates back to the 1430s. The existing house and buildings date from 1730, and now form the centrepiece of the 143 acre Park, which contains a handsome Craft Village. The Park, as well as being a craft, antique and garden centre, is still a working farm.

Hoar Park Craft and Antique Centre was established in 1994. This unique craft village has 17 craft shops, with the Granary Antiques Centre, featuring 12 antique dealers under one roof, new for 1998. Set in rolling wooded countryside, yet not far from the surrounding towns of Nuneaton, Coleshill, Solihull, Tamworth and Kingsbury, this delightful centre offers giftware, kitchen and tableware, old pine and Indonesian furnishings, a cabinet maker and wood turner, picture gallery and frameworks, needlecraft, cane chair restoration, hand-made chocolates, hand-painted and Tiffany lamps, candle fragrances, crystal giftware and engraving service,

Hoar Park Craft and Antique Centre, Ansley, Nr Coleshill Warwickshire CV10 0QU   Tel: 01203 394433.

pottery, ceramics and glassware, a stone mason, and a silversmith and jeweller, all in charming converted traditional farm buildings. Many of the craftspeople will accept commissions for custom-made items. There are also a garden centre and tea rooms adjacent, as well as a marvellous picnic and play area, children's farm, and country walks over the surrounding 146 acres. Country craft demonstrations and courses available throughout the year, as well as antiques & flea market in the summer months. Open Tuesday - Sunday, 10 - 5.

HARTSHILL   MAP 4 REF E3
3 miles NW of Nuneaton off the A5

Hartshill Hayes Country Park is an ideal place for exploring the developing rural attractions of this part of Warwickshire. Although surrounded by a network of roads, here visitors find only woodland trails and walks, and magnificent views. The park boasts 136 acres of woodland, meadow and open hilltop. Winner of the Forestry Authority's 'Centre of Excellence Award' in 1996, the park boasts three self-guided walks, an informative Visitors' Centre and truly wonderful views. Hartshill itself was the birthplace of the poet Michael Drayton (1563-1631).

   The Malt Shovel is a handsome whitewashed 18th-century public house carefully renovated and restored by proprietors Patrick and Lynda Mills, who have tastefully furnished it in old-world style. This large and welcoming former coaching inn is located between Nuneaton and Atherstone, close to the A5 and near Hartshill Hays Country Park, perfect for country walks through superb woodland. This Free House is popular with locals and also with the many walkers, ramblers and canal users who pass through (the Grand Union Canal is only ¼ mile away up the lane). A marina is currently under construction just up the road - an additional attraction for

**The Malt Shovel, 39 Grange Road, Hartshill, Nuneaton
Warwickshire CV10 0SS Tel: 01203 392501.**

the many visitors who come to sample the delights of this beautiful part of the county. Patrick and Lynda have been in the pub trade for 30 years, and are ably assisted by their son Richard, who acts as manager. They make every effort to ensure that guests have a relaxing and enjoyable time. There are meals on offer all day every day, ranging from traditional English roast grills to Chinese dishes and Indian curries, and 18 different puddings (popular favourites include Spotted Dick and rice pudding), all served in the lounge restaurant with full waitress service. The excellent food can be washed down with a choice of traditional real ales, wines or other beverages. Live music on Saturdays and Sundays.

WITHERLEY   MAP 4 REF E2
5 miles NW of Nuneaton off the A5

This is a charming village and makes a good stopping-off point where visitors can enjoy the rustic scenery and relax at one of the village's very good public houses.

MANCETTER   MAP 4 REF E2
5 miles NW of Nuneaton off the A5

This former Roman camp is situated on a rocky outcrop overlooking the valley of the River Anker. This camp was once one of a line of forts built by the Romans as they advanced northwards. The village is chiefly associated with the Mancetter Martyrs - Robert Glover and Joyce Lewis - both of whom were burnt at the stake for their religious beliefs. The martyrs are commemorated on wooden tablets in the fine **Church of St Peter**, which dates back to the early 1200s. The glory of this church is its rich glass in the east window of the chancel, most of which is 14th century in origin and thought to have been created by John Thornton, builder of the great east window of York Minster. Between the manor and the church are two noteworthy rows of almshouses dating from 1728 to 1822.

ATHERSTONE

Atherstone is a small market town situated on the Roman Watling Street at the eastern edge of the Warwickshire Forest of Arden, off the A5 between Nuneaton and Tamworth. Set against the wooded hills of the Merevale Estate, the picturesque town centre dates from medieval times and is unspoiled by modern development. The visitor will find a wealth of small, friendly shops and cafes, together with a good library and tourist information centre. Market days are Tuesdays and Fridays. The range of buildings on the east side of the Market Place reflects 500 years of English vernacular architecture.

Atherstone's history predates medieval times to the Anglo-Saxons; at the time of the Norman Conquest it belonged to the Countess of Mercia, Lady Godiva. The Domesday Book of 1086 records 14 residents: 11 villagers, two smallholders and one slave. Its importance as a trading centre grew and grew over the ensuing years, so that by 1724 Daniel Defoe could describe it as 'a town famous for a great cheese fair on the 8th September'.

Atherstone's **St Mary's Church** was founded in 1365 as a chapel-of-ease, becoming a parish church in 1835, when Atherstone separated from Mancetter to become a parish in its own right. The tower was rebuilt in 1782 in 'modern Gothic' style. To the rear of the building, the 12th century **Baddesley Porch**, brought from Baddesley Ensor church when the latter was demolished in 1842, boasts lovely decorative detail.

On Long Street, the main street of this attractive town, the **Hat & Beaver** is a distinguished public house in a handsome Georgian building. The clean lines and understated grace of the exterior speak of its early 18th century origins. Once the building had its own stabling to the rear, and a

The Hat & Beaver, 130 Long Street, Atherstone Warwickshire CV9 1AF Tel: 01827 720300.

blacksmith's. It became a public house in the mid-19th century. The pub takes its name from Atherstone's traditional role as a hat-making town. Beaver pelts were known to make the finest top hats. Owner Clive Pitts, after 25 years in the teaching profession, took over the running of his former local early in 1998. He offers all guests a warm welcome and genuine hospitality. Locals and visitors mix freely in this friendly and relaxed atmosphere. There's an ever-changing choice of real ales, with Worthington a permanent feature, plus Hair of the Dog, a brew made especially for this pub.

The **Atherstone Town Trail**, outlining a marvellous walk through the town and environs, is produced by Atherstone Town Council Hertiage sub-committee, and available from the town library.

NORTH AND WEST OF ATHERSTONE

GRENDON   MAP 4 REF E2
3 miles NW of Atherstone off the A5

Grendon once boasted its own mint, owned by Sir George Chetwynd of Grendon Hall. It was this same Sir George who fell in love with the actress Lillie Langtry, and who fought Lord Lonsdale in a fist fight to win her favour. He led an extravagant life, spending a lot of time at race meetings and entertaining the Prince of Wales, with the result that his beloved Lillie began a liaison with the Prince, and Sir George lost so much money that Grendon Hall had to be sold off; it was pulled down in 1933.

BADDESLEY ENSOR   MAP 4 REF E2
3½ miles W of Atherstone off the A5

Just across from Grendon, divided by the old turnpike road, Baddesley Ensor boasts a five-sided pulpit in the Wesleyan chapel, retrieved from the ancient church when it was demolished in 1842. This black pulpit is claimed to be the one from which the Protestant Bishop Latimer preached nearly 400 years ago; the Bishop was burned at the stake during Mary Tudor's reign. In 1772, when given the freedom to worship, Baddesley Quakers built a meeting house; up until earlier this century Quakers from many parts of the country made a yearly pilgrimage here.

BAXTERLEY   MAP 4 REFE2
3 miles W of Atherstone off the A5

This scenic and tranquil village has a handsome village green and pond. The **Rose Inn** is a large and hospitable pub and restaurant set alongside this village green and the banks of the village pond. This welcoming family-run concern is a popular retreat for locals and visitors alike, including the village ducks, who wander in from the pond to sample the delights of this pub's friendly atmosphere. Built in 1746, there is an extensive garden and play area. The pub boasts its original beams in its small but spacious rooms, with comfortable furnishings and a collection of advertising and animal prints adorning the walls. Two rooms have log fires. The food is

**Rose Inn, Main Road, Baxterley, Nr Atherstone
Warwickshire CV9 2LE Tel: 01827 713939.**

wholesome and home-cooked, offering a range of traditional favourites as well as curries and vegetarian options. There is a good choice of real ales and New World wines. Owner John Edwards and his family make every effort to ensure good and friendly service to every customer.

WARTON
MAP 4 REF E2

5 miles NW of Atherstone off the M42

This lovely village, though not far from the M42 motorway, is set amid rolling countryside and is a true haven of peace and tranquillity, affording some lovely views out over the rural landscape.

The Fox & Dogs is a traditional pub in a handsome whitewashed listed building adorned with flourishing hanging baskets of flowers and dating back to the late 18th century. Located in this pretty village, it offers a

The Fox & Dogs, Orton Road, Warton, Warwickshire B79 0HT
Tel: 01827 892448.

welcoming and hospitable haven for travellers. After many years of experience in the trade, Jacqueline and Garry Bennett came here in 1996 in their first venture as tenants. The interior is very attractive, with exposed brick walls and fire surround, lots of countryside prints adorning the walls and a magnificent display of gleaming brass implements and ornaments. Snacks and light meals are available until 6 p.m., including a range of traditional and more innovative dishes. Ales on offer include Marstons Pedigree, Marstons Smooth Brewed and Banks Mild, as well as Guinness and draught lagers and ciders. To the rear there's a large garden, which is a real sun trap during the summer months.

NEWTON REGIS   MAP 4 REF E1
6 miles NW of Atherstone off the B5453

One of the most unspoilt villages in Warwickshire, Newton Regis has been voted *Best Kept Small Village* on numerous occasions. Near the Staffordshire border and between the M42 and B5453, this lovely village is built around an attractive duck pond which was once a quarry pit. The village's name is thought to derive from its former royal ownership, having once been the property of King Henry II. It has in its day also been known as King's Newton and Newton-in-the-Thistles - the latter perhaps referring to the abundance of thistles or specially grown teasels which were used in the carding of flax fibre. Linen looms were worked in the house which is now the Queens Head Inn.

The Queen's Head was also once a coaching inn and dates back over 450 years. Always a hub of the local community, this very attractive whitewashed brick public house is beautifully decorated throughout, with exposed beams and a wealth of memorabilia on display. Leaseholder Michael Rhodes has over 21 experience in the licensing trade, but this is

**The Queen's Head, Main Road, Newton Regis, Warwickshire B79 0NF
Tel: 01827 830271.**

the first time that he and wife Debbie have been completely at the helm, having come here in 1997. They have met with great success, and take pride in upholding the pub's thriving reputation for quality and service. Yvonne is the excellent cook; lunch is available from 12-2 p.m., dinner from 6-9 p.m. (from 7 p.m. on Sundays), with a choice from the menu or the eight daily specials, including vegetarian meals. The excellent choice of ales available include Bass, Brew XI, Worthington Creamflow, Caffrey's,

Bass Mild and a guest ale which changes every fortnight. There is a lovely display of beer badges around the bar, depicting the number of ales that have been available here since Michael and Debbie's arrival.

FREASLEY   MAP 4 REF D2
5 miles W of Atherstone off the M42/A5

This tiny village boasts true rural elegance and some lush greenery. Here visitors will find **Planters Garden Centre**. After a number of years selling plants from a trailer at the side of the road, owners Gerald and Christine Ingram, opened this lovely establishment in 1991. Located in this lush part of the country the centre has been built from scratch on a green field site. Since opening it has expanded year on year and now covers six acres with plans in place for another expansion in 1999 in order to double the indoor space available. All plants here are bought in from leading nurseries, many of them local. The range of plants available is very impressive.

Gerald and Christine and their helpful, knowledgeable staff offer a full cross-section of plants and shrubs, all neatly arranged, for visitors to browse among at leisure. Also within the site is a wonderful aquatics section and large bonsai area. Many other items are available at this distinguished garden centre, including giftware, greeting cards, gardening tools, garden ornaments and more, as well as a wonderful Christmas display every year from mid-October through the end of December. The cosy coffee shop is just the place to relax and enjoy a quiet cuppa and a choice of hot meals, sandwiches, rolls and home-made cakes and pastries. This family-run establishment offers a good standard of service, including sound advice for gardeners at every level of experience, from beginners to past masters of the gentle art of gardening. Open Monday-Saturday 9 a.m.-6 p.m.; Sundays 11 a.m.-5 p.m.

**Planters Garden Centre, Woodlands Farm, Freasley
Warwickshire B78 2EY Tel: 01827 251511 Fax: 01827 262440.**

ALVECOTE   MAP 4 REF E2
6 miles NW of Atherstone off the M42

Alvecote Priory, just on the border with Staffordshire, was formed by William Burnett in 1159, who built it as a penance after having (mistakenly) believed that his wife had been unfaithful during his pilgrimage to the Holy Land. This small Benedictine Priory was founded as a Cell to the Great Malvern Priory in Worcestershire. As with many others it was dissolved in 1536, when the buildings were converted into a house, which was pulled down in about 1700 when another house was constructed using some of the old materials. The 14th century remains include a fine moulded doorway and dovecote.

Alvecote Priory Picnic Area boasts canalside picnic spots and a nearby nature reserve. There is also an interesting circular walk that takes in lakes, wildlife, many unusual plants, the old North Warwicks Colliery tip, and handsome canal bridges.

AUSTREY   MAP 4 REF E1
7 miles NW of Atherstone off the M42

This handsome village contains some very fine timbered houses and cottages, some of them thatched and is well worth taking the time to visit.

MARKET BOSWORTH   MAP 4 REF F2
7 miles NE of Nuneaton off the B585

Britain in Bloom winner for the years 1995-1998 and just over the county border in Leicestershire lies Market Bosworth. This market town is of course most famous as the battle site for the turning point in the Wars of the Roses - Richard III (Duke of York, the 'White Rose' county) was routed here by 'Red Rose' forces (Henry Bolingbroke, later Henry IV, of Lancaster) and killed in 1485. This was the battle immortalised in Shakespeare's play Richard III, where the king is heard to cry 'My kingdom for a horse.' Richard's defeat led to the reign of the Tudor dynasty, Shakespeare's patrons and perhaps, therefore, the impetus behind his less-than-complimentary portrayal of Richard, which is disputed by historians to this day. Today's Market Bosworth occupies a delightful rural setting, offering many opportunities for good walks and gentle recreation.

For that unique personalised gift, **Bosworth Crafts** is well worth a look. This distinctive shop specialises in handcrafted leatherwork. Owner Roy Thorley designs and works the pieces by hand - handbags, purses, wallhangings, rocking horse saddles and bridles - and will customise any piece to the buyer's personal tastes, as well as offering an extensive range of his own exclusive designs. Here in this delightful rural setting, this cottage

**Bosworth Crafts, 23 Main Street, Market Bosworth
Warwickshire CV13 0JN Tel: 01455 292061.**

cum shop also sells high-quality glassware, figurines, pottery and greeting
cards, as well as work by master sculptor John Letts of Nuneaton, creator
of the statue of George Eliot that graces Nuneaton town centre.

4 Central Warwickshire

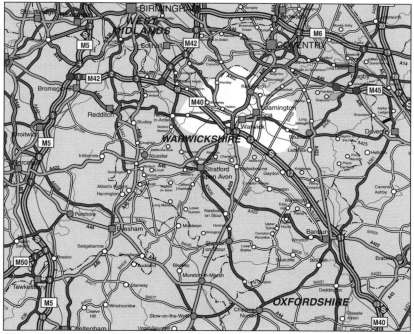

© MAPS IN MINUTES ™ (1998)

A rich vein of medieval and Tudor history runs through the heart of Warwickshire. The romantic ruins of Kenilworth Castle, the grandeur of Warwick Castle, and the elegance of Leamington Spa set the tone for this most delightful part of the county.

The Norman Conquest saw the establishment of Warwick Castle as a royal stronghold, in order to keep the local population under control. The 18th century saw the redesign of country estates, including Capability Brown's work at Warwick Castle itself.

At the close of the 18th century, Leamington began to develop as a spa. Not far away in distance but a world away in the social hierarchy of the time, Joseph Arch was born in 1826 at Barford. A pioneer of the farm workers' union movement and later an MP, the Joseph Arch Inn at Barford must be one of the few pubs in England to be named after a trade union leader.

Welcome, then, to a land of castles and cottages, of historical intrigue and modern comforts. Welcome to England's historic heartland.

KENILWORTH

Although the town was here before the Domesday Book was compiled, Kenilworth's name is invariably linked with its castle. Today the remains of this castle stand as England's finest and most extensive castle ruins, dramatically ensconced at the western edge of the town.

Kenilworth Castle's red sandstone towers, keep and wall glow with an impressive richness in the sun, particularly at sunrise and sunset. Here you can learn about the great building's links with Henry V (who retired to Kenilworth after the Battle of Agincourt), King John, Edward II and John of Gaunt. The tales of this great fortress, immortalised (if enhanced)

Kenilworth Castle

in Sir Walter Scott's novel *Kenilworth* written in 1821, are many and varied.

The marvellous Norman keep, the oldest part of the ruins, was built between 1150 and 1175. John of Gaunt's Great Hall once rivalled London's Westminster Hall in palatial grandeur. After Simon de Montfort's death at the Battle of Evesham in 1265, Kenilworth was held by his son. At that time the castle was surrounded by the Kenilworth Great Pool, a lake covering about 120 acres. Henry VIII's army failed in its attempts to storm the castle by using barges to cross the lake. Eventually the castle fell, after six months' siege, when starvation forced de Montfort to surrender.

Some 300 years later Elizabeth I visited Kenilworth, then held by her favourite the Earl of Leicester. The Earl had much adapted the existing fortress, and laid on celebrations for the visiting monarch costing around £60,000, in which the Queen was welcomed by the Lady of the Lake, floating on the waters of the Great Pool.

Leicester's neglected wife Amy Robsart died nearby in mysterious circumstances (it was never ascertained whether her fall down a flight of stairs was murder, accident or suicide). The Virgin Queen was compelled by the resulting controversy to distance herself from Leicester, whom she eventually had executed for treason.

An audio tour guides you on a revealing journey around the Castle, recounting stories of Kenilworth's turbulent past. There are fine views from the top of Saintlowe Tower, and lovely grounds for exploring and picnicking, as well as beautifully reconstructed Tudor gardens. Special events throughout the year include a festival of Tudor Music, Saxon and Viking exhibitions, medieval pageantry, various re-enactments, plays and operas in the grounds and much more.

The remains of Kenilworth's abbey can be seen in the churchyard of the Norman parish church of **St Nicholas** in the High Street. Much of interest was discovered during excavations and there are many relics on display in the church, including a pig made of lead. It is said that this formed part of the roof at the time of the Dissolution, but was then melted down and stamped by the Commissioners of Henry VIII.

For those who'd like to stay on to be able to explore Kenilworth more fully, **Victoria Lodge Hotel** is a welcoming family-run hotel/bed and breakfast located in a large and attractive Victorian home which has been refurbished to a high standard of taste and comfort. To the rear there is a walled garden established in the 1850s. Breakfast is served outdoors in fine weather, under a pergola of vines and clematis. The atmosphere throughout is peaceful and relaxed. The nine guest rooms (one with four-poster bed) are decorated with many individual pieces, including some hand-made by owners Chris and Trevor Woolcock's family. The guests'

**Victoria Lodge Hotel, 180 Warwick Road, Kenilworth
Warwickshire CV8 1HU Tel: 01926 512020 Fax: 01926 858703.**

lounge is cosy and just the place for a relaxing drink at the licenced bar. Among the many individual and distinctive features of this handsome establishment are the collections of English pottery and Australian prints (the latter reflecting the Woolcocks' Antipodean origins).

AROUND KENILWORTH

ASHOW   MAP 3 REF E5
1½ miles E of Kenilworth off the B4115

Avon Cottage in Ashow, at the far end of this attractive village adjacent to the Church is a charming cottage garden surrounding a picturesque 18th-century Grade II listed building. It stretches for 1½ acres with extensive River Avon frontage. Diverse and interesting plantings make for year-round interest. There is also an attractive orchard area with free-range domestic hens and waterfowl.

HONILEY   MAP 3 REF D5
4 miles W of Kenilworth off the A4177

Honiley is a lovely conurbation with the feel of a village imparted to it by its handsome 18th century church.

WARWICK

Over the past ten centuries **Warwick Castle** has witnessed some of the most turbulent times in English history. From the era of William the Conqueror to the grand reign of Queen Victoria, the Castle has left us a fascinating legacy to enjoy today. Dominating the town, it is surely everyone's ideal of a medieval building, one of the country's most splendid castles and certainly one of the most visited. It still serves as a home as well as retaining the greater part of its original masonry.

Standing by the River Avon, Warwick is in a good defensive position and became part of Crown lands as recorded in the Domesday Book in 1086. Much of the castle was destroyed during the Barons' revolt in 1264, led by Simon de Montfort, and the majority of the present castle dates from the 14th century. The towers at each end are very impressive - one is known as Caesar's Tower and is shaped rather like a clover leaf.

A tour of this palatial mansion takes you from the grim austerity of the original dungeons with their gruesome torture chambers to the gloomy but sumptuous opulence of rooms later adapted for comfortable living. The castle's magnificent State Rooms, once used to entertain the highest members of the nobility, house some superb art treasures including works by Holbein, Rubens and Velasquez. As the castle is owned by Madame Tussaud's, striking waxworks take their part in the displays. The Royal Weekend Party 1898 leads us into the social whirl, hidden intrigues and gracious decorum of Daisy, Countess of Warwick and her 'Marlborough Set'. Another display, occupying the 14th century undercroft, recreates the medieval household's preparations for battle. Known as the 'Kingmaker' attraction, it recreates life in the 15th century with vivid realism, depicting a scene hours before the final battle of Richard Neville, Earl of Warwick (known as 'Kingmaker' for helping successive kings, both Yorkist - as in the case of Edward IV - and Lancastrian - with Henry VI - to lay claim to the English throne). It was in fighting the deposed King Edward's troops in 1471 that the Earl was killed.

In the castle's Ghost Tower, visitors can learn of the dark and sinister secrets surrounding the fatal stabbing of Sir Fulke Greville, said to haunt the premises to this day. In the Great Hall visitors come face to face with Oliver Cromwell's death mask. And the armoury houses one of the best private collections in the country.

The castle exterior is best viewed from Castle Bridge, where the 14th century walls can be seen reflected in the waters of the River Avon. There is a walk along the ramparts, and much to explore within 60 acres of grounds, including a re-created Victorian formal rose garden, the Peacock Gardens and an expanse of open parkland designed by Capability Brown.

Events throughout the year include Medieval Tournaments, open-air fire-work concerts and special entertainment days.

A strong link with the castle is found in the **Collegiate Church of St Mary** in Old Square, a splendid medieval church on the town's highest point. Of pre-Conquest origin, the church contains the magnificent fan-vaulted Beauchamp Chapel, built to house the monuments of Richard Beauchamp, Earl of Warwick, and his family. The chapel houses an out-standing collection of Warwickshire tombs, a chapter house and a Norman crypt (complete with a tumbrel, part of a medieval ducking stool). In summer visitors can ascend the tower to enjoy the excellent views.

Giovanni's is a charming and welcoming restaurant in Warwick town centre, near the castle. Featured in 'The Good Restaurant Guide', where it is awarded the highest rating, this convivial establishment offers all the flavour and variety of authentic Italian cuisine.

The attractive interior is decorated Sicilian-style, with original paint-ings on the walls. The menu features home-made pasta dishes; specialities include fresh fish, veal, steaks made with Scottish Angus beef, and vegetar-ian options. All the produce used is fresh daily. There is an extensive wine list featuring wonderful Italian vintages; a range of Italian beers is also on offer. Most of the delicious Italian desserts are home-made. For a taste of genuine Italian cooking, this congenial establishment is hard to beat.

Giovanni's, 15 Smith Street, Warwick, Warwickshire CV34 4JA
Tel: 01926 494904.

The Zetland Arms is a welcoming and attractive public house located in a handsome Georgian building with charming casement windows and a mews-style frontage. Located on Church Street in the old town centre of Warwick - the street taking its name from the proximity of the fine Church of St Mary's, just a few steps away from the pub - and only 200 metres from Warwick Castle, this distinguished establishment is popular with local residents, businesspeople and visitors alike.

Rebuilt in the early 1700s after the Great Fire of Warwick in 1694, the interior is traditional through and through, with framed paintings of the Castle, and scenes of Warwick, gracing the walls. The delightful walled garden at the rear seats 100 people and is adorned with hanging baskets

**The Zetland Arms, Church Street, Warwick, Warwickshire CV34 4AB
Tel: 01926 491974.**

are filled with beautiful flowers and foliage, enhancing the graceful charms of this fine establishment. The meals (lunch only) feature English home cooking presided over by Darren himself, an Egon Ronay Pub Chef of the Year. The extensive selection of wines and champagne are available by the glass or bottle, and there are also Davenports and Bass real ales on tap. This graceful and elegant pub is the perfect place to go for a relaxed drink or meal in genteel surroundings. And should you decide to prolong your stay in this part of the county, the Zetland Arms also has five guestrooms available.

The centre of Warwick was rebuilt after a fire in 1694. Though many older buildings survived, the centre is dominated by elegant Queen Anne rebuilding. A walk around High Street and Northgate Street takes in some of the finest buildings, including Court House and Landor House. Court House on Jury Street houses the **Warwickshire Yeomanry Museum**, with displays of uniforms, arms, swords, sabres and selected silver, and **Warwick Town Museum**, which features changing exhibitions.

Some of the town's oldest structures can be found around **Mill Street**, an attractive place for a stroll, with several antique shops along the way. The **Mill Garden** at the end of Mill Street is home to a delightful series of plantings in a breathtaking setting on the Avon beside the castle. Here visitors will find a herb garden, raised beds, small trees, shrubs and cottage plants including some unusual varieties.

As its name betokens, **The Cellar Restaurant** in the heart of historic Warwick occupies an underground chamber redolent with history and a truly unique ambience. Here in this subterranean hideaway, with the stone arches of the cellar rising in a semicircle overhead, the atmosphere is cosy and intimate. The exposed brick walls and stone slab flooring enhance the feeling that one is dining in a secret haunt known only to a select few. Situated off Smith Street in The Knibbs, a small alleyway which once led to a courtyard, it is entered on street level. Diners then descend the stairs into this atmospheric and very stylish restaurant. For owners Richard and

**The Cellar Restaurant, The Knibbs, Smith Street, Warwick
Warwickshire CV34 4UW Tel: 01926 400809.**

Faye, this lovely establishment is a labour of love; Richard, an experienced and highly qualified chef, has worked all over the world. Faye tends to front of house, bringing years of experience to her personable and genuinely friendly demeanour.

The menu is outstanding, and changes seasonally. There is an accent here on Mediterranean-style dishes, though there is also a tempting range of traditional English and European specialities. The wide choice ensures that there is something to please every palate, from the home-made Provençal-style fish soup to the maize-fed chicken breast and mouth-watering desserts. Other tempting dishes from the vast and varied array are roast saddle of wild boar, freshly grilled tuna steak, and Scotch fillet of beef. All dishes are prepared and presented with great style, as befits this elegant establishment. The well-stocked bar has a fine range of wines, spirits and other liquid refreshment to accompany the excellent food. When the weather permits, there is also an outdoor dining area on the lovely, flower-filled terrace. Open lunch and evening Tuesday-Saturday, for lunch only Sunday. Booking advised.

The Doll Museum, Warwick

Warwickshire Museum in Market Place occupies a 17th century market hall housing collections that illustrate the geology, wildlife and history of the county. Notable exhibits include giant fossils, live bees, ancient jewellery and the historic Sheldon Tapestry map of Warwickshire. Changing programmes in the ground floor galleries offer exciting exhibitions of acclaimed local and national artists' work.

History of a different kind can be seen at picturesque **Oken's House**, an ancient building once owned by Thomas Oken, a self-made businessman who died childless in 1573 and left his fortune to found almshouses for the poor. Today his home houses **The Doll Museum**, just 100 yards from the castle in Castle Street. This carefully restored Elizabethan house is home to hundreds of dolls, teddies and toys from days gone by. Visitors can have a go at hopscotch or spinning tops, or hunt for Teddy's friends, while video bring the exhibits to life, demonstrating how all the mechanical toys on display work.

Lord Leycester's Hospital, Warwick

One of the most important buildings in Warwick is **St John's House**, dating from 1666 and considered a very good example of the period. Today the building houses a museum where visitors can find out how people lived in the past. The displays include a gallery of costume, a kitchen full of drawers to open and cupboards to explore, a parlour, and a schoolroom just waiting for Victorian children. Upstairs there is the **Museum of the Royal Warwickshire Regiment**.

Two of Warwick's medieval town gateways survive, complete with chapels. Of these, Westgate Chapel forms part of **Lord Leycester's Hospital**, a spectacularly tottering and beautiful collection of 15th century half-timbered buildings enclosing a pretty galleried courtyard. Inside, the main interest is provided by the Queen's Own Hussars regimental museum. This 600-year-old medieval treasure has a unique chantry Chapel, magnificent Great Hall and Guildhall together with other timber-framed buildings, first established by the Earl of Leicester as an old soldiers' home in 1571. The candlelit chapel dates from 1123, and the Regimental Museum of the Queen's Own Hussars is another site of interest in this medieval masterpiece. The historic Master's Garden, featuring a Norman arch and 2,000 year-old vase from the Nile, is a spectacular summer attraction.

In the heart of Warwick, just 400 yards from the castle, the **Lord Leycester Hotel** occupies Grade II listed buildings steeped in history: In 1694 they halted the Great Fire of Warwick; in the 1700s they housed the Three Tons Inn; and by the 19th century they were elegant townhouses.

**Lord Leycester Hotel, Jury Street, Warwick, Warwickshire CV7 4EJ
Tel: 01926 491481**

In 1925 the hotel was founded, and has remained a focus of Warwick society, as when it was used as an American Officers' Club during the Second World War. This traditional and tasteful hotel has recently been refurbished to a high standards of comfort and elegance. Pictures and paintings of Warwick, the castle, and a history of the Earls of Warwick down through the centuries adorn the walls, and there is wood pannelling and other graceful period details throughout.

The restaurant offers excellent value table d'hote lunches and dinners, with a menu that changes daily. The full a la carte menu makes a feature of seasonal produce. Traditional English breakfast and afternoon tea is also available, and bar snacks are on offer in the lounge throughout the day. The choice of quality wines is extensive. Each of the 48 bedrooms is individual, reflecting the character of a building with over 300 years of history. They are furnished to ensure guests' every comfort. This distinguished and extensive hotel has facilities for business travellers which include conference suites, syndicate rooms and a board room. It also makes an ideal location for special occasions such as weddings, christenings and other parties. Justly famous for the standard of service, the friendly and helpful staff make every effort to ensure that guests' every requirement is provided for quickly and efficiently. Any stay here is sure to be a relaxing and highly enjoyable one.

All in all, Warwick is one of the most complete historic towns in the country. Guided walks around the town are conducted by members of the Warwick Society. Contact the Tourist Information Centre in Jury Street for details.

Warwick Racecourse in Hampton Street offers flat and steeple chase racing throughout the year. This picturesque racecourse makes for a good day out for all the family, with a regular programme of 25 meetings throughout the year. The central grandstand incorporates the first stand built in 1809, among the oldest surviving in the country.

The Vine Inn is a very attractive public house and restaurant located just south of the town centre of Warwick, near Westgate Tower and some 400 metres from the Racecourse. Occupying a lovingly restored 15th century building, and retaining the original beams (and its own resident ghost!), this spacious and handsome pub has traditional furnishings and a small gallery of photographs and prints of local places of interest and historical scenes. There is a good selection of hearty English main courses, making the most of fresh local produce, all home-cooked, to be followed by a traditional pudding and washed down with one of the excellent real ales, beers, or wines on offer.

In winter guests can enjoy a relaxing drink in front of the real log fires; on fine days they can make use of the outdoor seating. Proprietor Sue English and her staff offer the many visitors to this popular establishment

**The Vine Inn, West Street, Warwick, Warwickshire CV34 6AW
Tel: 01926 490744.**

a friendly welcome and efficient, conscientious service. Open all day 7 days a week.

AROUND WARWICK

HATTON   MAP 3 REF D5
2½ miles NW of Warwick off the A41

Hatton Country World is a uniquely charming blend of family fun and country shopping. On this 100 acre farm, visitors will find the largest collection of rare breed farm animals in Britain and the largest craft village in England.

The farm was built by descendants of Sir Richard Arkwright of Spinning Jenny fame. As farming methods changed, the small cows' stalls, granary and carthorse stables became impractical, so a new use for them was found. The old 19th century buildings were converted into craft workshops. This award-winning craft village today houses an extraordinary grouping of craftsmen and -women: some 35 workshops employing over 100 people. In this flourishing centre visitors will find workshops with jewellery, knitwear, ceramics, handmade furniture, toys, an art gallery, candlemakers and much more. It now comprises some three dozen workshops; other enticements include the restaurant, cafe and bar, garden centre, farm shop, and 'one-stop animal shop'. Children get to feed and stroke the animals for hours in Pet's Corner, and Guinea Pig Village is not to be missed. The adventure playground attractions start with the simple activity centre and lead up to the commando slide, 'Fortress Hatton' and trampoline certain to keep them happy for hours.

The Farm Park has a serious educational side too, maintaining a constant programme to inform and educate the public about farm life. There are also sheep dog displays, a falconer in residence, and a nature trail that leads to the longest flight of canal locks on the Grand Union Canal at Shrewley.

SHREWLEY   MAP 3 REF D5
5 miles NW of Warwick off the B4439

Shrewley boasts a marina is situated on the **Grand Union Canal**. Its well-known landmark is the Hatton flight of 21 locks that stretches for 2½ miles up Hatton Hill.

CLAVERDON   MAP 3 REF D6
6 miles W of Warwick off the A4189

Claverdon is spread over a wide area now, but there is evidence of a medieval village enclosed in a deer park during the 14th century. All that now remains to mark the site is Park Farm, which is near the church with its 15th-century 'embattled' tower. In the church there are some fine monuments to the Spencer family.

Dating back to the 16th century and a pub for over 200 years, **The Red Lion at Claverdon** has long occupied a special place at the heart of local community life. People come from all parts of the county and further afield to this high-quality pub/restaurant. Offering lovely views south to

The Red Lion at Claverdon, Station Road, Claverdon
Warwickshire CV35 8PE Tel: 01926 842291 Fax: 01926 842167
Website: www.web-sites.co.uk/redlion

the Cotswolds and the Malvern Hills, this restful and welcoming establishment has carefully restored original oak beams and other traditional features. The front room is bedecked in sunny Mediterranean colours, as owners David and Jackie Ward used to run a successful restaurant in Spain, and the Spanish influence makes itself felt in the restaurant's decor and menu. Dishes on offer include tasty starters and a choice from among at least 10 main courses, featuring lamb, chicken, fish, seafood, pasta, and beef, all freshly prepared with an emphasis on fresh produce lovingly and carefully prepared. There is a good range of real ales, including a guest beer, and a selection of wines. Meals are served 7 days a week: Monday to Saturday noon-2.30, 7 - 9.30; Sundays two lunchtime sittings (noon and 2pm) and from 7 - 9 pm, with a choice of three roasts . Reservations advised for Friday and Saturday evenings and Sunday lunch.

Woodside Country Guest House is the picture of peace and comfort here in this picturesque and rural village. This secluded cottage-style house has lovely woodland walks that begin right on the doorstep, as well as acres of garden. The 5 guest bedrooms are comfortable and spacious; all afford views of the garden, orchard and woods. There is also a sunny guests'

Woodside Country Guest House, Langley Road, Claverdon Warwickshire CV35 8PJ Tel: 01926 842446.

sitting room overlooking the garden. Proprietor Doreen Bromilow has run this attractive bed and breakfast for 20 years, and brings the benefit of her experience to making every guest's stay both enjoyable and truly relaxing. She is also an accomplished naturalist painter and embroiderer, and her works adorn this gracious and charming home from home.

ROYAL LEAMINGTON SPA

This attractive town boasts a handsome mixture of smart shops and Regency buildings. **The Parade** is undoubtedly one of the most handsome street in Warwickshire. It starts at the railway bridge, dives between a double row of shops and comes up again at the place marked with a small stone temple announcing 'The Original Spring Recorded by Camden in 1586'. In 1801 very few people knew of the existence of Leamington, but by 1838 all this had changed. By this time the famous waters were cascading expensively over the many 'patients' and the increasingly fashionable spa was given the title 'Royal' by permission of the new Queen, Victoria. The Pump Rooms were opened in 1814 by Henry Jephson, a local doctor who was largely responsible for promoting the Spa's medicinal properties. This elegant spa resort was soon popularised by the rich, who came to take the waters in the 18th and 19th centuries.

Immediately opposite the Spa itself are **Jephson's Gardens** containing a Corinthian temple which houses a statue of him. The town's supply of saline waters is inexhaustible, and a wide range of 'cures' are available, under supervision, to this day.

Just a short walk from the centre of historic Royal Leamington Spa, in Clarendon Avenue, **Winstons** is a grand and lively public house. Deceptively small from outside, the interior is surprisingly extensive and supremely comfortable. This dynamic establishment serves a good range of ales including Boddingtons, Flowers IPA, Guinness and Boston Beer, as

Winstons, 44/46 Clarendon Avenue, Royal Leamington Spa Warwickshire CV32 4RZ Tel: 01926 339433.

well as a variety of fine ciders, lagers, wines and spirits. The wooden and stone-flagged floors are a feature in this cosy and attractively decorated pub. Well known for its atmosphere and friendly ambience, it is open evenings only from 6 p.m. Monday-Friday, and from 4 p.m. at weekends. Owner Chris Jarrett has run the pub since 1996, and has taken care to inject a real sense of fun and hospitality into this attractive pub. He and his staff make every effort to ensure that guests have an enjoyable and relaxing time. The individual tables encourage guests to enjoy a chat or sample the musical entertainment on offer most weeknights, which ranges from 80s favourites to DJ-mastered dance music.

Warwick District Council Art Gallery and Museum in Avenue Road boasts collections of pottery, ceramics and glass, as well as some excellent Flemish, Dutch and British paintings from the 1500s to the present.

Leamington Spa also makes an excellent base for exploring the surrounding countryside, Warwick, and Stratford-upon-Avon.

Known as Warwickshire's premier seafood restaurant, **Ocean Bar and Restaurant** is a modern, vibrant establishment in Leamington Spa town centre, just off Warwick Street. The restaurant area is situated above the bar and comprises two galleries connected by a bridge. Done in minimalist style and seaside fresh blues and white, with attractive lighting and contemporary furnishings, it cites as its inspiration the long sleek finishes of New York and the chic minimalism of contemporary London.

Ocean Bar and Restaurant, 44 Oxford Street, Leamington Spa Warwickshire CV32 4RA Tel: 01926 422224.

In this dynamic setting, an exciting range of imaginative and tempting dishes are served, such as smoked haddock tortellini with lobster sauce, pan-fried dover sole with green lentils, spring salad and sauce vierge, and seared swordfish steak with tomato risotto and orange-flavoured jus, to name but three. This contemporary menu combines the best of British and European influences, and there is also an extensive selection of spirits and distinguished French wines. Open noon-3pm and 7-10.30pm. Complimentary tapas at the bar from 5-7pm.

Close to the town centre, shops and the famous Bowls Club, **Trendway Guest House** offers a relaxing and very comfortable place to stay for visitors to this part of the county. Owners Kenneth and Pauline Sloane bought this attractive Victorian townhouse in early 1998, and have altered and improved it with great care and attention to detail. The seven spacious ensuite rooms (including two family rooms) in this 2-crown rated estab-

**Trendway Guest House, 45 Avenue Road, Leamington Spa
Warwickshire CV31 3PF Tel: 01926 316644.**

lishment are light and airy. The guests' lounge is welcoming and cosy, and there is also an attractive breakfast area. Guests have a choice of full English or Continental breakfast, home-prepared. This popular guest house is always busy, so pre-booking is strongly advised.

UFTON FIELDS NATURE RESERVE
3 miles SE of Leamington Spa off the B4452

MAP 3 REF F6

This haven is open every Sunday from 11 a.m.-4 p.m. It boasts an all-weather footpath and a wealth of butterflies, dragonflies and wild flowers, as well as a bird hide. It is well worth a visit for all those interested in the natural history and wildlife of this part of Warwickshire.

HARBURY
4 miles SE of Leamington Spa off the B4452

MAP 3 REF F6

The history of this area goes back many years; dinosaur fossils have been found in the local quarries and the Fosse Way, a major Roman road, passes close by. Just outside the village lies **Chesterton Windmill**. This unusual mill was built in 1632 and was the work of Inigo Jones.

5 Stratford-upon-Avon & South Warwickshire

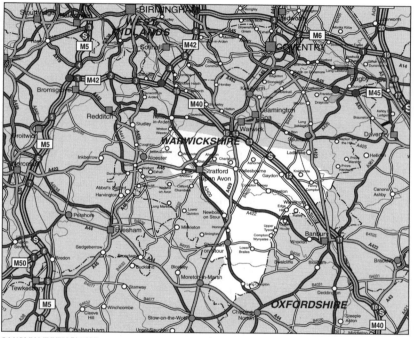

© MAPS IN MINUTES ™ (1998)

While Stratford will be the obvious focal point for most visitors to this part of Warwickshire, the region boasts any number of attractive and peaceful villages and hamlets well off the beaten tourist track. As well as a wealth of attractive vistas visitors can view the stately manor of Charlecote, the impressive art collections at Upton House and the newly re-opened Compton Verney, the Nickelodeon at Ashorne with its unique collection of mechanical musical machines, and, for those interested in engineering feats of a uniquely British persuasion, the Heritage Motor Centre at Gaydon.

Southern Warwickshire's waterways form an important and extensive part of the 2,000 miles of Britain's inland network, boasting as it does long stretches of the Oxford Canal, as well as restored lengths of the Stratford Canal and the upper Avon. This part of the county was also the scene of the first major battle of the English Civil War - at Edgehill in 1645. As will be seen, there are many delights to treasure in this part of Warwickshire, quite apart from the outstanding cultural and historic treasures in Stratford-upon-Avon itself, particularly around the extreme southern edge of the county, which skirts the Cotswold Scarp and is dotted with the distinctive ochre-coloured ironstone cottages indigenous to this part of the world.

STRATFORD-UPON-AVON

After London, for many visitors to England Stratford-upon-Avon is the next place on their itinerary, and all because of one man. William Shakespeare was born here in 1564 , found fame in London and then retired here, dying in 1616. This place, where he was born and where he grew up, is dominated by the great playwright and poet. Needless to say, the places connected with his life and work have become meccas for anyone interested in the cultural history, not just of these islands, but of the entire world.

Each of the houses associated with the Bard has its own fascinating story to tell. Staff at the houses are happy to guide visitors on a journey encompassing what life might have been in Stratford-upon-Avon during Shakespeare's day.

Shakespeare's Birthplace, Stratford-upon-Avon

Some 500,000 people each year visit **Shakespeare's birthplace** alone, located in the very centre of the town, in Henley Street. The house in which he was born and where he grew up remained in the ownership of Shakespeare's family until 1806. The timber-framed building contains the exhibition *William Shakespeare: His Life and Background*, a lively and comprehensive introduction to his life and work. On display within the house are rare examples of furniture and needlecraft from the 16th century. The garden is designed in traditional style, and boasts plantings, including shrubs, herbs and flowers, mentioned in the great man's works.

Further along, on Chapel Street, stands **Nash's House**. This half-timbered building was inherited by Shakespeare's grand-daughter, Elizabeth Hall, from her first husband, Thomas Nash. It now contains an exceptional collection of Elizabethan furniture and tapestries, as well as displays, upstairs, on the history of Stratford. The spectacular Elizabethan-style knott garden is an added bonus to this excellent site. Next door, in **New Place**, Shakespeare bought a house where he spent his retirement years, from 1611 to 1616. Today all that can be seen are the gardens and foundations of where the house once stood. An exhibit in Nash's House explains why this, Shakespeare's final home in Stratford, was destroyed in the 18th century. Opposite New Place is the **Guild Chapel**, and beyond this is the **Grammar School**, where it is believed that Shakespeare was educated.

Hall's Croft in Old Town is one of the best examples of a half-timbered gabled house in Stratford. It was named after Dr John Hall, who married

Hall's Croft, Stratford-upon-Avon

Shakespeare's daughter Susanna in 1607. Dr Hall ran a successful medical practice here, treating patients rich and poor. It is believed that John and Susanna Hall lived here until her father's death, when they moved into New Place. This impressive house contains outstanding 16th and 17th century furniture and paintings. There is also a reconstruction of Dr Hall's 'consulting room', accompanied by an exhibition detailing medicinal practices during Shakespeare's time. Outside, the beautiful walled garden features a large herb bed; visitors can take tea near the 200 year-old mulberry tree or have lunch in the restaurant here.

Hall's Croft is near **Holy Trinity Church**, an inspiration for many poets and artists because of its beautiful setting beside the River Avon. It is here that Shakespeare is buried. Dating partly from the 13th century, it is approached down an attractive avenue of limes. The north door has a sanctuary knocker, used in the past to ensure any fugitive who reached it 37 days' grace. Shakespeare's wife Anne Hathaway and their daughter Susanna and her husband John Hall are also buried here. The tomb of the great man himself carries a sobering inscription:

> *Good friend, for Jesus sake, forbeare*
> *To digg the dust enclosed heare;*
> *Blese be ye man yt spares these stones*
> *And curst be he yt moves my bones.*

Shakespeare is not the only illustrious name to have associations with the town. **Harvard House** in the High Street, dating from 1596, was the childhood home of Katherine Rogers. Her son, John Harvard, went to the American Colonies in the early 1600s and founded the famous university named after him in 1636. In 1909 Harvard House was restored and presented to Harvard University. It boasts the most ornately carved timbered frontage in the town. Cared for by the Shakespeare Birthplace Trust, it houses the nationally important Neish Collection of Pewter.

There are many fascinating old buildings in Stratford. The old market site in Rother Street has a history dating from 1196, when a weekly market was granted by King John. In the square is an ornate fountain-cum-clock tower, a gift from G W Childs of Philadelphia in the jubilee year of Queen Victoria. It was unveiled by the famous actor Henry Irving, who when knighted in 1895 became the first ever *'Sir of the Stage'*.

Stratford has become a mecca for theatre-lovers, who flock to enjoy an evening at one of the town's three theatres. On the walls of **The Dirty Duck** public house is a gallery of glossy signed photographs of famous faces. These are some of the actors and actresses who have who have appeared at the **Royal Shakespeare Theatre** just across the road. This attractive pub with its famous customers sums up Stratford: it manages to go about its busy normal life while thousands of visitors arrive from all over the world each year.

The first commemoration of Shakespeare's passing was organised by the actor David Garrick (of Garrick Theatre and the Garrick Club fame), 150 years after Shakespeare's death. People have been celebrating this illustrious poet and playwright's life and times ever since.

The site of 17/18 High Street was once owned by the Guild of the Holy Cross, and has seen much history from its early days as an Elizabethan town house to its present incarnation as a distinguished restaurant and bistro.

The Royal Shakespeare Company has an unrivalled reputation both in the UK and worldwide. Wherever the RSC perform, the audience are certain of witnessing performances of a high standard. The company has operated in its present manner since 1961, but the history of Stratford and theatres goes well before this. The first permanent theatre was built as a result of local brewer, Charles Edward Flower, who gave a two-acre site on which to build a theatre in Shakespeare's birthplace in 1875, and then launched an appeal for funds.

This theatre opened in 1879 with a performance of Much Ado About Nothing starring Ellen Terry and Beerbohm Tree. The season was limited to one week as part of a summer festival. It was so successful that, under the direction of F R Benson, it grew to spring and summer seasons, touring the nation in between. In 1925, because of the excellence of the performances and direction, the company was granted a Royal Charter. Sadly, a year later the theatre perished in a fire. At the time, playwright George Bernard Shaw sent a one-word telegram: Congratulations! Apparently the building was a bit of an eyesore, but there are few such buildings in today's Stratford.

The company, undeterred, continued by giving performances in cinemas while a worldwide fundraising campaign was launched to build a new theatre, which was opened on 23rd April, 1932, the 368th anniversary of the Bard's birth.

A tour of the RSC theatre gives visitors the opportunity to discover what goes on behind the scenes. The itinerary for tours varies according to rehearsal schedules and the technical work underway on stage, but they are very informative and fun, and usually include both the Royal Shakespeare and Swan Theatres, as well as the RSC Collection - with over a thousand items on view, including costumes, props, pictures and sound recordings depicting changes in staging from medieval times to the present. The displays compare and contrast theatrical productions past and present, giving an insight into the many interpretations adopted and styles used in the presentation of great works of classical drama over the years.

Only 10 minutes' walk from the centre of Stratford (motorists can follow the one-way system, taking the Warwick Road, then turning left at St Gregory's Church into Welcombe Road. At the top of this road, the hotel is on the right), **Stratford Court** is a distinguished country house hotel set in an acre of walled gardens, with views over the Welcombe Hills. This impressive Edwardian house retains many of its original features and much

Stratford Court Hotel, Avenue Road, Stratford upon Avon Warwickshire CV37 6UX Tel: 01789 297799 Fax: 01789 262449.

of its traditional character and charm. There are 12 guest bedrooms, all ensuite, and all furnished in keeping with the rest of the house, with an abundance of oak and antiques, enhancing the hotel's warm, comfortable and welcoming ambience. The principal bedrooms have wonderful oak four-poster beds. Guests are welcome to enjoy a relaxed drink in the Garden Bar, which affords wonderful views over the extensive grounds, or in the supremely comfortable lounge with its open fireplace. Breakfast is served in the oak-floored dining room, which also features oak shuttered windows. Three-course dinners can also be taken here by prior arrangement.

A short walk from the centre of town are the Bancroft Gardens, near the 14-arch Clopton Bridge. This delightful leisure area contains the great **Shakespeare Memorial**, designed by Lord Ronald Gower and built in Paris. The work took 12 years to complete and was finally presented to the town in 1888. Only a few yards away is a preserved industrial tram, employed on the horse-drawn tramway connecting wharfs in Stratford with those in Shipston-on-Stour and Moreton-in-the-Marsh in Gloucestershire. The canal was completed in 1816.

The **Ashley Court Hotel** is a comfortable and pristine establishment offering bed and breakfast accommodation. This large and welcoming Vic-

Ashley Court Hotel, 55 Shipston Road, Stratford upon Avon Warwickshire CV37 7LN Tel: 01789 297278 Fax: 01789 204453.

torian building is set in an acre of mature gardens which lead to the 'Tramway walk', which takes walkers past the cricket ground and butterfly farm and into the theatre gardens and the centre of Stratford, after just 6 or 7 minutes' walk. Owners Joan and Ian Charman make every effort to ensure guests' comfort and enjoyment. There are 10 beautifully decorated rooms, all ensuite; two feature four-poster beds. Full English or Continental breakfast is served in the dining room, which seats 30 and also offers pre-theatre dinners; the adjacent bar and patio are relaxing places to enjoy a quiet drink.

Quite apart from the industry that has grown around Shakespeare and his life and times, Stratford boasts a number of other world-class attractions.

Stratford's **Butterfly Farm** is on Tramway Walk. Here, a specially designed and constructed habitat makes the perfect home for Europe's largest collection of butterflies. This indoor exotic tropical rainforest boasts rare blooms, waterfalls and fish-filled pools. Hundreds of the world's most spectacular and colourful butterflies fly around in perfect freedom. Visitors can observe close to the butterflies' life-cycle. There is also an area devoted to Insect City, where stick insects, beetles, leaf-cutting ants, bees and many more of nature's miracles can be seen. And for the brave of heart, Arachnoland is home to the deadly and dangerous spiders of the Amazon and elsewhere. Here, the world's largest spider, rainforest scorpion colonies and other 'spinners' can be seen in perfect safety.

The Ragdoll Shop on Chapel Street was created by the founder of Ragdoll Productions, which produce the charming and popular children's television series Rosie and Jim. For the uninitiated, are ragdolls who ply the canals in their decorative canal boat, the Ragdoll, with their owner, who makes up stories about them along the way. Unbeknowst to their owner, Rosie and Jim also come to life and enact their own adventures! The shop devotes over half its floor space to play areas for children. There is also a wealth of books, videos and other merchandise which can be purchased, including guides to water safety produced by British Waterways, which runs the two-centuries-old network of canals and inland waterways in England, Scotland and Wales, conserving the canalside historic buildings and structures, and protecting the wildlife and plantlife along the water's edge. British Waterways work closely with Ragdoll Productions, to produce among other things children's water safety information.

Stratford's **Teddy Bear Museum** occupies an original Elizabethan setting on Greenhill Street. The collection comprises hundreds of wonderful teddy bears from around the world - including some of the oldest, most valuable and most unusual to be found.

The Royal Shakespeare Theatre Summer House on Avonbank Gardens is home to the **Stratford Brass Rubbing Centre**, which contains a large collection of exact replicas of brasses of knights and ladies, scholars, merchants and priests of the past. Admission is free; a small charge is made for the special paper and wax required.

Guided walks which explore Shakespeare's life in Stratford are available, beginning and ending at the RSC Swan Theatre on Waterside. This two-hour walk places the life and times of the man in the context of his historic surroundings.

River cruises are available from Stratford Marina with Maydawn Cruises, which plies canal boats along the Avon to pass the towns, villages and countryside, much of which remains unchanged since Shakespeare's day. Both all-day (eight-hour) and half-day (four-hour) cruises are on offer.

AROUND STRATFORD-UPON-AVON

SHOTTERY   MAP 3 REF D7
1 mile W of Stratford off the A422

This was the birthplace of Anne Hathaway, Shakespeare's wife. Here visitors will find the Elizabethan farmhouse now known as **Anne Hathaway's Cottage**, and can retrace the steps which the courting couple, who married in 1582, might have taken. The epitome of the traditional thatched

Anne Hathaway's Cottage, Shottery

cottage, this delightful spot has been home to Hathaways since the 15th century, up until some 70 years ago when the Shakespeare Birthplace Trust decided it was time to open up the home to the public. The Hathaway bed, settle and other pieces of furniture owned by the family remain, and there is a traditional English cottage garden and orchard - plants and herbs grown by the Shakespeare Trusts' gardeners can be purchased. Other attractions of this handsome village are the Shakespeare Tree Garden, the tranquil Shottery Brook, and well-laid-out Jubilee Walks.

WILMCOTE
3 miles NW of Stratford off the A34

MAP 3 REF D6

Another notable house connected with the poet is that of his mother, situated here in the village of Wilmcote, slightly off the well-beaten tourist track. **Mary Arden's House** is a striking Tudor farmhouse. Guided tours are available and the house boasts the Shakespeare Countryside Museum of farming and rural life. Note in particular the bread oven doors, which are made of bog oak, which never burns, and are seen only very rarely now in England. Special events and demonstrations of traditional sheep shearing, weaving and spinning, crook making and other country crafts are held throughout the year, as well as celebrations and entertainments based on accounts from Shakespeare's plays, in particular his A Winter's Tale.

Best of all, however, is the dovecote of the house. Robert Arden, who was lord of the manor, was in this capacity the only villager allowed to have one. It has over 600 pigeon holes and, at nesting time, would house about 3,000 birds.

Wilmcote is also one of the few small villages left which retains its Victorian Gothic railway station. The Stratford Canal runs alongside the railway. After many years of neglect, the Canal was taken over by British Waterways and now carries many holiday cruisers on their way to join the Avon.

ASTON CANTLOW   MAP 2 REF C6
5 miles NW of Stratford off the A3400

This handsome village boasts timbered houses and an impressive Guild-hall, as well as a lovely church where Shakespeare's parents were married.

BISHOPTON   MAP 3 REF D6
1½ miles N of Stratford off the A46

Here in this sleepy hamlet, a world away from the bustle of Stratford just a mile and a half distant, comes an opportunity to relax in a most peaceful rural setting.

On the edge of Bishopton hamlet, **Burton Farm** is a 16th century Tu-dor farmhouse with former barns that have been renovated to create handsome and relaxing bed and breakfast accommodation. This family-

Burton Farm, Bishopton, Stratford upon Avon
Warwickshire CV37 0RW Tel: 01789 293338.

run B&B is set within a 150 acre corn, sheep and beef farm. The farmhouse's provenance is evidenced by the exposed beam timbers in the main rooms and the flagstone floors. There are antique furnishings and paintings in the guests' lounge, dining room and hall. The farmhouse and barns are surrounded by lovely mature gardens with pools which support many different species of wildlife, birds and rare plants. There are five very comfortable and attractive guestrooms, four ensuite and one with private bath, including a family room which sleeps five. One room has a marvellous four-poster bed. The full English or Continental breakfast is hearty and filling. Owners Eileen and Tony Crook are friendly and conscientious hosts, offering guests a genuinely warm welcome. Children welcome.

ALVESTON

MAP 3 REF D6

2 miles NE of Stratford off the B4086

This charming village on the River Avon boasts several lovely cottages and two wonderful churches - and just five minutes from Stratford. The **Ferry Inn** occupies a large and rambling whitewashed building dating back to the 17th century. With its casement windows and other original features, this welcoming establishment has a genuinely cosy and peaceful ambi-

**The Ferry Inn, Ferry Lane, Alveston, Stratford upon Avon
Warwickshire CV37 7QX Tel: 01789 269883.**

ence. Just two minutes' walk from the River Avon, it is set in a lovely village with charming cottages and two lovely churches - all just five minutes from Stratford. This traditional inn has open fires in winter, and very comfortable seating. There are picnic tables and umbrellas outside, overlooking the village green, for enjoying a quiet pint on fine days. The traditional English a la carte menu features Aberdeen Angus steaks, gammon, liver and bacon and other traditional favourites. Fish dishes are a speciality with Monkfish, Hake and Tuna, as well as vegetarian meals, excellent salads, home-made pies and puddings. Portions are generous and the service is friendly and efficient. There is also an extensive range of real ales and good wines. Advance booking is advised.

CHARLECOTE   MAP 3 REF E6
3 miles E of Stratford off the B4086

The National Trust's **Charlecote Park** is a magnificent stately home occupying extensive grounds overlooking the River Avon. Home of the Lucy family since 1247, the present house was built in the mid-16th century; Thomas Lucy was knighted here by Robert Dudley, Earl of Leicester, deputising for Elizabeth I, who spent two nights here in 1572. The house was comprehensively modernised during the 18th century, but when George

**Charlecote Park, Charlecote, Nr Stratford upon Avon
Warwickshire CV35 9ER Tel: 01789 470277
email vclgri@smtp.ntrust.org.uk**

Hamilton Lucy inherited it in 1823 he took the decision to 'turn the clock back' and create interiors according to rich Victorian 'Romantic' ideals of the Elizabethan era. The house, apart from the family wing which is still used by descendants of these early Lucys, has not been changed since. The lavish furnishings of the house include important pieces from William Beckford's Fonthill Abbey sale in 1823. A treasure-trove of historic works of sculpture and painting, no visitor can fail to be impressed by the house's sheer magnitude, grace and beauty. The park was landscaped by 'Capability' Brown and reflects his use of natural and man-made features complementing each other. The park supports herds of Red and Fallow deer (in about 1583 the young William Shakespeare is alleged to have been caught poaching Sir Thomas' deer; years later he is said to have taken his revenge by using Sir Thomas as his inspiration for the fussy Justice Shallow in The Merry Wives of Windsor), as well as a flock of Jacobs sheep first introduced here in 1756. Special events are held throughout the year; at any time a visit to this national treasure is an assured lovely and informative day out.

Charlecote Mill is situated on the site of an earlier mill mentioned in the Domesday Book, at which time it was valued at six shillings, eight pence. In 1978 this 18th century building was restored with the help of volunteers from Birmingham, and the west waterwheel was repaired at the expense of the BBC for their film of George Eliot's novel, The Mill on the Floss.

ASHORNE   MAP 3 REF E6
5 miles NE of Stratford off the B4100

Here at **Ashorne Hall** visitors will find the 'Mighty Cinema Organ Show' as well as guided tours of the world-famous Nickelodeon Collection of Mechanical Music, England's rarest collection of mechanically-played instruments. The collection includes music boxes, demonstrations of self-playing harps, violins, accordions, drums, magic pictures that come to life, fairground organs, life-sized automata figures and huge dance organs. The site also hosts special musical tea parties, dinner dances and Christmas parties. Outside, visitors will encounter the beautiful Victorian gardens and a narrow-gauge steam/diesel railway.

WELLESBOURNE   MAP 3 REF E6
6 miles E of Stratford off the A429

Wellesbourne Wartime Museum is located on the site of a wartime airfield. On display are tools, ration books and an exhibit in the style of a contemporary battle operations control room.

The **Wellesbourne Watermill** is a genuine brick-built working flour mill dating back to 1834. This restored mill on the River Dene, a tributary of the River Avon, is one of the few in the country which visitors can see working as it did over 160 years ago. A video presentation prepares visitors for the mill itself, providing an insight into this heritage site.

Demonstrations of the art and skill of milling stoneground flour are enacted and explained by the miller, and visitors are encouraged to take part. Apart from the working demonstrations, there are guided walks alongside the river and two ponds, tree trails, and coracle boats along the river. There is also a display of antique farm implements, a craft shop, and a tea room in the wonderful 18th century timber-framed barn where teas and

**Wellesbourne Watermill, Kineton Road, Wellesbourne
Warwickshire CV35 9HG Tel: 01789 470237 Fax: 01789 841540
email: ahamilton@wellesbournemill.demon.co.uk**

lunches are served. Local paintings and local produce are on sale - and, of course, freshly ground flour. Open 10-4.30 April-September Thursday to Sunday and Bank holidays; school holidays (late July-early September) Tuesday to Sunday.

COMPTON VERNEY   MAP 3 REF E7
6 miles SE of Stratford off the B4086

Before crossing the Fosse Way, the Roman road that runs from Exeter to Lincoln passes **Compton Verney Manor House**. For many years closed to the public, this magnificent manor has been renovated so that now the house and much of its fine collection are open to the public. This exquisite collection features works of art brought together for the first time, many never before seen by the general public. The collection, which is still growing, includes British portraiture, European Old Masters and modern works, along with a unique assemblage of British Folk Art. Workshops, evening talks, lectures and special events bring to life the processes and inspiration behind some of these great works.

The manor house stands amid 40 acres of parkland landscaped by Capability Brown and rich in flora and fauna, with a lake, arbour, stirring stone obelisk, Victorian watercress bed, Cedar of Lebanon, and Adam Bridge. The handsome avenue of Wellingtonias line what was once the entrance to the estate.

GAYDON

MAP 3 REF F7

6 miles E of Stratford off the B4100

The Heritage Motor Centre in Gaydon hosts the world's largest collection of historic British cars, together with outdoor activities for the whole family. This fascinating Centre tells the story of the British motor industry from 1896 to the present day. It boasts about 200 exclusively British vehicles from the world-famous makes of Rover, Austin, Morris, Wolseley, Riley, Standard, Triumph, MG and Austin Healey. This 65 acre site also features a 4 x 4 off-road demonstration circuit.

KNIGHTCOTE

MAP 3 REF F7

8 miles E of Stratford off the B4451

Knightcote is a quiet and relaxing village boasting some excellent walking along a tributary of the River Itchen. Situated within a 500 acre working farm, **Knightcote Farm Cottages** are three lovely self-catering cottages created from renovated and handsomely refurbished former agricultural buildings. Making an ideal base from which to explore Leamington Spa, Warwick, Stratford and the many delightful villages and towns in the area, the cottages are cosy, comfortable and equipped with every modern convenience. The decor and furnishings capture the essence of country living, from the antique French or country pine beds to the solid English oak and ash kitchen units.

Knightcote Farm Cottages, The Bake House, Knightcote Nr Leamington Spa, Warwickshire CV33 0SF Tel: 01295 770637 Fax: 01295 770135 website: www.knightcotefarm.mcmail.com email: fionawalker@mcmail.com

One cottage is particularly equipped for disabled guests, including specially designed sink and worktop units which can be hired and installed to suit an individual's precise requirements. One cottage sleeps four, the others sleep six. Opened in 1997, this family-run enterprise is the labour of love of partners Richard and Anne Renfrew and Craig and Fiona Walker, who work hard to ensure that guests have a rewarding, enjoyable and memorable stay. The views in every direction are outstanding, and the surrounding countryside is perfect for relaxing, tranquil walking. Winner of the 1998 Self-Catering of the Year Award for the Heart of England. English Tourist Board Highly Commended.

FENNY COMPTON   MAP 3 REF F7
11 miles E of Stratford off the A423

This charming village close to **Burton Dassett Hills Country Park** and just half a mile from the Oxford Canal provides endless opportunities for scenic walks along the edge of the Cotswold Scarp. Burton Dassett Park itself is distinguished by rugged open hilltops topped by a 14th century beacon with marvellous views in all directions.

The Merrie Lion is a charming, family-run public house in this very scenic village. Here at the southern extremity of the county and not far from Farnborough Hall, it is popular with locals, walkers, ramblers, and canal-users. Built in 1710 of local Hornton Stone, its name was changed 40 years ago to include 'Merrie', the name of the then-owner's daughter. This delightful establishment is the epitome of a cosy country pub: exposed beams, three small rooms and real log fires in winter; there is also

The Merrie Lion, High Street, Fenny Compton
Warwickshire CV33 0YH Tel: 01295 770881.

outdoor seating for when the weather is fine. The real ales available include Banks's and Wadsworth 6X; there is also a good range of other beers, wines, spirits and soft drinks. The menu includes eight main courses plus steak and chicken specials at weekends - all freshly cooked. There are also good-value sandwiches, toasties and home-made soups on offer.

KINETON
MAP 3 REF E7
7 miles SE of Stratford off the B4086

This market town is a peaceful retreat with an old Courthouse and several 17th and 18th century houses. The church tower dates from the 14th century, the rest having been rebuilt around 1755.

EDGE HILL
MAP 3 REF F7
9 miles SE of Stratford off the B4086

Here in 1642, the first and distinctly not decisive battle of the Civil War took place. Initially the Royalist cavalry routed the opposition, but a lack of discipline saw their advantage lost. The Castle Inn pub stands above the battlefield, and is reputedly the point where Charles I's standard was raised.

RATLEY
MAP 3 REF F7
9 miles SE of Stratford off the B4100

Ratley lies in the folds and valleys over the crest of the Edge Hill on the border of Oxfordshire. The inhabitants will tell you that it is both the oldest and the highest village in Warwickshire and that, during the Second World War, from the hill that leads up from the village the fires of both London and Birmingham could be seen as they blazed after German bombing. The cottages in this lovely village are built of the distinctive yellow/ochre ironstone indigenous to these 'border' villages.

WARMINGTON
MAP 3 REF F7
9 miles SE of Stratford on the B4100

The National Herb Centre enjoys a great location on the northern edge of the Cotswolds on the B4100 close to the Warwickshire-Oxfordshire border. A centre for research and development work for the UK herb industry, the site has been developed with an eye towards providing visitors with a fascinating range of activities and sights. The Plant Centre has one of the widest selections of plants, trees and shrubs with herbal uses in the country. The Herb Shop stocks a range of herbs, health foods and gifts, many produced on site.

The Herb Bistro offers lunches, teas and refreshments. There are display gardens designed by Chelsea Gold Medallists Simon and Judith

**The National Herb Centre, Banbury Road, Warmington, Nr Banbury
OX17 1DF Tel: 01295 690999.**

Hopkins, and an Exhibition of herbs and their uses through the ages. The
nature trail affords some marvellous views across the valley as well as a
chance to observe native wildlife close to, including foxes, roe deer, woodpeckers and muntjac. The friendly staff are only too willing to offer help
and information. The site is open 1st March-31st October 9.30-5.30; No-
vember-December 9.30-dusk.

UPTON HOUSE   MAP 3 REF F8
9 miles SE of Stratford off the A422

Here on the border with Oxfordshire, **Upton House** is a late 17th century
National Trust property built of the mellow local stone. The house was
remodelled in 1927-9 for the second Viscount Bearsted, to house his growing art collection and also to modernise the premises. The collections in
the house are the chief attractions, featuring paintings by English and
Continental Old Masters such as El Greco, Brueghel, Bosch, Hogarth and
Stubbs. Brussels tapestries, Sèvres porcelain, Chelsea figures and 18th-cen-
tury furnishings are also on display. In the fine gardens, in summer there
can be seen the typically English scene of white-clad cricketers; in winter,
the Warwickshire hunt hold their meet.

COMPTON WYNYATES   MAP 3 REF E8
8 miles SE of Stratford off the A422

The outstanding **Compton Wynyates** manor is an estate which has been
in the same family since the 13th century. Sir William Compton built this
magnificent manor, and it remains a fine example of Tudor redbrick construction.

UPPER TYSOE
MAP 3 REF E8
8 miles SE of Stratford off the A422

From Upper Tysoe there is a lovely walk south over Windmill Hill (which actually has a windmill on it), taking you to the church on the edge of Compton Wynyates park, with views of the attractive Tudor manor below - a refreshing bit of brick building in this Cotswold-edge stone country.

HONINGTON
MAP 3 REF E8
7 miles SE of Stratford off the A3400

Honington Hall encapsulates the architectural and decorative styles popular in the late 17th and 18th centuries. Opening times are limited but the Hall is well worth a visit, presenting many delightful examples of Regency tastes and refinements.

SHIPSTON-ON-STOUR
MAP 3 REF E8
8 miles SE of Stratford off the A3400

For centuries, Shipston-on-Stour was an important agricultural centre, in the heart of a rural district known as 'Feldon'. From the 1200s tradesmen and craftsmen helped shape the town that remains to this day a centre for fascinating shops, galleries and antiques shops. The hills that surround the town are perfect for gentle strolls and cycling. This small town has quite a busy shopping centre, but is rewarding to stroll through, with a nice church and many handsome old stone buildings.

LOWER BRAILES
MAP 3 REF E8
11 miles SE of Stratford off the B4035

The George Hotel dates back to 1350 and was built, so it is believed, to house the masons who built the marvellous **St George's Church** nearby, with its graceful slender spire. The village also boasts some pretty stone houses and nice views.

LONG COMPTON
MAP 3 REF E9
12 miles SE of Stratford off the A3400

Just a short distance from the Oxfordshire border, this handsome village lies close to the local beauty spot known as Whichford Wood. It is a pleasant Cotswold village of thatched stone houses and some antique shops.

In the village itself visitors will find **The Manor House**, an impressive and distinctive hotel with a long and distinguished history. Situated at the southern tip of Warwickshire in the heart of the Cotswolds, this picturesque and evocative 16th century hotel offers a taste of gentile country

**The Manor House Hotel, Main Street, Long Compton
Warwickshire CV36 5JJ Tel: 01608 684218.**

life. Surrounded by exquisite mature gardens, the hotel is built of Cotswold stone and has leaded windows with heraldic stained glass. There are
five lovely ensuite rooms, TV lounge, reading room, bar and attractive
dining room seating 28. Guests are welcome to make use of all 26 rooms,
as if at home. The dining room offers a full a la carte menu for guests and
non-residents, bar snacks, and full English breakfast. Sunday lunches are a
speciality, featuring Aberdeen Angus beef. An ideal base for the Cotswolds,
Blenheim Palace, Stratford, Hidcote Gardens and the historic Rollright
Stones, just 1½ miles east, the village itself has many idyllic delights,
including the genuine lych-gate in the village churchyard. For a truly luxu-
rious experience, look no further. Restaurant open for lunch 7 days a week,
for dinner Mon-Sat. ETB 3 Crowns Commended, AA 3Qs.

A mile or so to the south of Long Compton, straddling the Oxfordshire border, are the **Rollright Stones**, made up of the King Stone on one
side of the lane, with the other two stone groupings - known as the King's
Men and the Whispering Knights - on the other. Legend has it that this
well-preserved stone circle is a king and his men, tricked by a sorceress
into falling under her spell, and then petrified.

6 Solihull and South West Warwickshire

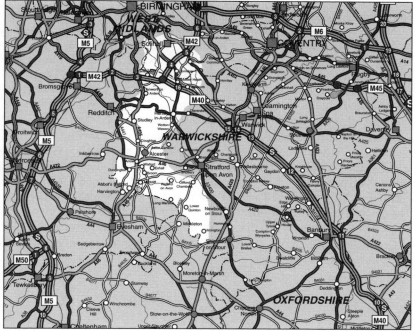

This chapter follows part of the *'Heart of England Way'* running south, from the remains of the historic Forest of Arden to the northeastern edge of the Cotswolds. As might be expected, this part of Warwickshire is rich in rural delights. Village after village along the Rivers Avon, Arrow or Alne, many relatively untouched since Tudor times, reflect some of the best traditional architecture and scenery to be found in the region, and contribute to Warwickshire's status as the *Heart of England*. There are also several impressive hilltop views to be had along the way, revealing breathtaking views of the surrounding countryside.

This part of the county also boast two very different but equally impressive stately homes: Coughton Court and Ragley Hall. Both of these distinctive country manors maintain fine collections, the amassed rewards of centuries of taste, power and wealth.

Other highlights of the region include picturesque gardens, peaceful woodland walks and a wealth of well-kept timbered and half-timbered houses, some constructed from centuries-old Arden oak.

SOLIHULL

Solihull began life as a sparsely populated village in a relatively underpopulated part of the country. It did not begin to grow in size, industry and importance until the 1930s. Its motto - 'urbs in rure' (town in country) - is well deserved. Its cottages and houses, since medieval times, have always blended in well with the greenery which covers a large swathe of the surrounding region. Today, Solihull's existing 17th and 18th century houses clearly demonstrate the good planning which has always been a hallmark of this town's social and architectural design.

Solihull's **church of St Alphege in the Square** was a favourite of John Constable's, who used to come here regularly to sketch the enchanting window tracery, foliage and corbels in the 13th century chancel. The beautiful Chantry Chapel of St Alphege was built in 1277 by Sir William de Odingsells, who employed a priest just to pray for the souls of his parents. The priest took his work home with him, as it were, his lodgings being the crypt below, in which a fireplace was installed to keep him warm.

Solihull also makes an excellent base from which to explore several gems in the immediate area.

AROUND SOLIHULL

KNOWLE   MAP 2 REF D4
1½ miles SE of Solihull off the A4141

The Elizabethan **Grimshaw Hall** in Knowle is a fine example of a carefully restored building of great historic significance. Nearby **Chester House** was built in the mid-14th century; it has been successfully refurbished and is today used as library, thus offering a practical service to today's population.

DORRIDGE   MAP 2 REF D5
2 miles S of Solihull off the A3400

This pretty suburb of Solihull is home to **The Forest Hotel**, which has been owned by the Muntz family for over 120 years. Located amid rolling countryside yet handy for the centres of Warwick, Stratford and Birmingham, as well as local National Trust properties, it makes for a peaceful,

**The Forest Hotel, Station Approach, Dorridge, Solihull
Warwickshire B93 8JA Tel: 01564 772120.**

relaxing haven. Opposite Dorridge Railway Station, on the Chiltern line, it is just as accessible for travellers without cars as for those with their own transport. The 12 recently refurbished ensuite rooms are tastefully furnished and offer a high standard of comfort and quality. The cosy lounge bar, cocktail bar and public bar are very attractive, and offer a good variety of draught beers and lagers, including real ales. Bar snacks, lunch and afternoon teas are served in the lounge bar (Monday-Saturday). The excellent Spinney Restaurant (open Monday-Saturday 6-8.30) features an imaginative menu and a good range of daily specials, with an emphasis on fresh local produce. The traditional Sunday lunch is very popular, and deservedly so. Guests are always made most welcome in the warm and comfortable atmosphere of this superior hotel.

The Railway Tavern, known locally in this lovely village simply as The Tavern, has been in the same family since 1913. Joe and Janet Watson carry on the family tradition with great style, maintaining the pub's welcoming atmosphere and reputation for great food and ales. Dating back to the coming of the London-Birmingham Great Western Railway line, it was prior to this two cottages - one a cobbler's and the other that of a herbalist and sweetmaker - before becoming an inn. Located on the outskirts of Dorridge, it is very cosy and welcoming.

Beautifully decorated throughout, it offers a comfortable and relaxing retreat to all its guests. There is a range of meals available from the menu and the changing specials board, with traditional favourites such as homemade cottage pie to more innovative dishes such as whole partridge cooked in cider. In season it is renowned for its game dishes. There are always at

**The Railway Tavern, Grange Road, Dorridge, Nr Solihull
Warwickshire B93 8QA Tel: 01564 773531.**

least four real ales available, including Brew XI and Bass, as well as a good
selection of lagers, ciders and wines. To the rear there is a wonderful garden, seating up to 200 people and incorporating a safe children's play
area.

EARLSWOOD   MAP 2 REF C5
4 miles SW of Solihull off the B4102

This very handsome village is located amidst scenes of rural tranquillity.
Here the weary traveller will find **The Bull's Head** public house and restaurant, offering a warm welcome in gracious surroundings, replete with

**The Bull's Head, Limekiln Lane, Earlswood, Solihull
Warwickshire B94 6BU Tel: 01564 702335 Fax: 01564 700022.**

atmosphere, excellent facilities and genuine hospitality. The pub occupies a large mid-18th century whitewashed building that has been a pub since the early 1800s. Completely refurbished early in 1998, it now boasts a very stylish appearance while retaining its historical roots: half-panelled walls, part quarry-tiled and part-wooden floors, and old prints depicting the locality adorning the walls, are testaments to its traditional appeal. Licensees Andrew and Claire, who have run this delightful pub since April 1998, have created a friendly, lively ambience which attracts a large and loyal following of locals and visitors. They maintain a high standard of service and quality. The restaurant menu offers a wide range of traditional and more innovative dishes; real ales on hand include Tetleys and Speckled Hen, plus a changing guest ale. The pub is open all day seven days a week; in the restaurant, lunch is served 12-3 daily, dinner 6-11 p.m. daily.

HOCKLEY HEATH   Map 2 ref D5
5 miles S of Solihull off the A3400

Pretty Hockley Heath is the village nearest the impressive **Packwood House**, lying in the Forest of Arden. This handsome timber-framed house began life in the 16th century as a farmhouse. It was renovated in the mid-17th century, and latterly carefully repaired, restored and enhanced by Graham Baron Ash, the donor of the property to the National Trust in 1941. It stands as an outstanding 20th century evocation of domestic Tudor architecture.

The house has a fascinating collection of furniture, tapestries, needlework and works of art. The garden topiary is justly famous: Carolean yews have been clipped to represent the Sermon on the Mount.

This charming village is also home to a world-class art and craft centre which also can provide accommodation. **Boxtrees Farm Art & Craft Centre** is an attractive bed and breakfast and art and craft shop complex set in traditional farm buildings which have been tastefully modernised. The farm was built early in the 18th century, and is now home to 13 individual shops. *Corner Cottage Picture Framing* offers a high quality of service. *The Farm Shop* has a range of fresh produce for sale. *KC Stained Glass* provide leaded lights, engraved windows and stained glass mirrors, clocks, Tiffany-style lampshades and made-to-order glasswork. *The Fabric Barn* has a wealth of materials for quilting, furnishings and other creative projects. *U-Me-Us* supply lovely hand-crafted candles, incense sticks, crystals and hand-forged ironwork.

Trooper Brown's is the place for specialist coffees from around the world, as well as a wide selection of coffee- and tea-making equipment - complemented by a wonderful range of Belgian chocolates and traditional sweets. *Stonecraft Garden Ornaments* supply a variety of pots, planters, bird baths

**Boxtrees Farm Art & Craft Centre, Stratford Road, Hockley Heath
Solihull B94 6EA. Farm Tel: 01564 782039 Fax: 01564 784661.**

and garden adornments. *Busy Lizzie's* offers fresh, dried and silk flowers
and personalised balloons for every occasion. *Wendy's Piece of Cake* make
delicious celebration cakes, all made on site and decorated to the customer's specifications. *The Hay Loft* sells decoupage prints, craft sets and
accessories as well as gifts and cards for all occassions. *Timeless Toys* specialises in making and restoring Rocking Horses, traditional wooden toys,
collectable Bears, Dolls Houses and accessories.

Visitors are invited to watch the craftsmen and -women at work, and
commissions are welcome. And after a morning's or afternoon's browsing,
Hiley's Coffee Shop is the place to relax and enjoy a quiet cuppa and deli-
cious cakes, snacks or lunch (open all day; lunch served 12-3 p.m.); on
Friday and Saturday evenings (7-10 p.m.) this attractive premises becomes
Hiley's Bistro, for a truly special dining experience. There is also bed and
breakfast accommodation available in the 18th century farmhouse. The
Centre is open Wednesday-Monday 10 a.m.-5.30 p.m.

LAPWORTH   MAP 2 REF D5
6 miles S of Solihull off the A3400

Here where the Grand Union and Stratford Canals meet, handsome
Lapworth boasts some characterful old buildings. Just outside the village
Baddesley Clinton is a romantic, medieval moated manor house which
has changed little since 1633. Set against the backdrop of the Forest of
Arden, this National Trust-owned property has had strong Catholic connections throughout its history. There is a tiny chapel in the house, and
secret priests' holes, used to hide holy fathers during the fiercely anti-
Catholic times during the reign of Charles I. The grounds feature a lovely
walled garden and herbaceous borders, natural areas and lakeside walks.

More modern additions to the site include the second largest ice rink in the country. Lunches and teas are available.

Off the A3400 between Hockley Heath and Henley-in-Arden, set in a peaceful lane and situated in two acres of picturesque grounds with commanding views over lovely countryside, **Lapworth Lodge Country Guest House** is a haven of peace and relaxation which makes an ideal base from which to explore all the sights and attractions of this part of Warwickshire. This former farmhouse was built in the 18th century, and has been extensively renovated to accommodate the needs of its guests. The seven

Lapworth Lodge Country Guest House, Bushwood Lane, Lapworth Warwickshire B94 5PJ Tel: 01564 783038 Fax: 01564 783635. Mobile: 01970 828341

ensuite rooms are large and very comfortable, with tasteful furnishings and decor; one boasts a four-poster bed. All offer a high standard of luxury and comfort. The breakfast area is pristine and, again, very charmingly decorated. The hospitality in this family-run guest house is excellent; owner Dawn Boucher takes real pride in meeting guests' every requirement, to ensure they have a relaxing, very pleasant and memorable stay. Open all year round.

TANWORTH-IN-ARDEN   MAP 2 REF C5
6 miles SW of Solihull off the B4101

In this pretty rural setting on the northwest edge of Warwickshire,

Umberslade Children's Farm in Tanworth-in-Arden is entered down a delightful avenue of poplars leading after a mile to this early 19th century farmhouse and outbuildings. Owned by the Muntz family since 1850, and a family-run working farm since 1951, it offers visitors a chance to sample the life, fun and information to be found in seeing sheep and lambs, goats and kids, pigs, ponies and many other animals in traditional agricultural buildings and settings. Popular with families, as well as walkers and ramblers enjoying the open spaces of nearby country walks, this educational

**Umberslade Children's Farm, The Leasowes, Tanworth-in-Arden
Warwickshire B94 5AE Tel: 01564 742251.**

and rewarding hands-on experience should not be missed. There are guided tours, farm walks and an adventure trail, as well as special seasonal events throughout the year, in particular lambing (March/April) and sheep-shearing. The farm/souvenir shop and excellent coffee shop are also worth a visit. Open daily mid-March-end September 10 a.m.-5 p.m., and weekends during October.

HENLEY-IN-ARDEN   MAP 2 REF C5
7 miles S of Solihull off the A3400

Possibly the finest old market town in Warwickshire, Henley-in-Arden's mile-long High Street is brimming with examples of almost every kind of English architecture from the 15th century onwards, including many old timber-framed houses built with Arden oak. Little remains today of the Forest of Arden, the setting adopted by William Shakespeare for his As You Like It, as its stocks were diminished in the 18th century by the navy's demand for timber, but nothing could diminish the beauty of Henley itself.

The town emerged initially under the protection of Thurston de Montfort, Lord of the Manor in 1140. Beaudesert Castle, home to the de Montfort family, lies behind the churches of St John and St Nicholas, where remains of the castle mound can still be seen. Famous visitors of the past to this delightful town have included Dr Johnson, his friend James Boswell, and the poet Shenstone.

The 15th century church of **St John the Baptist** has a tower which dominates the High Street where it narrows near the ancient **Guildhall**. The roof of the Guildhall is supported by oak beams which were growing at the time of the Norman invasion; a wooden candelabra hangs from the ceiling. At one end of the hall there is a huge dresser displaying a set of pewter plates dating back to 1677. The charter granted the town has a royal seal embossed in green wax, kept in its own glass case here in the Guildhall.

The town's Court Leet still meets yearly with the Lord of the Manor at their head, as they have for centuries. Members of this distinguished grouping have included the High Bailiff, Low Bailiff, Ale-taster (now there's a job!), Butter-weigher, the Mace bearer, the Town Crier, the Town constable, the Two Affearers and the Two Brook Lockers. In 1655 the meeting's minutes note, 'usually heretofore there have been at Henley-in-Arden several unlawful meetings of idle and vaine persons about this time of yeare for erectings of May Poles and May bushes and for using of Morris dances and other heathenish and unlawful customes, the observation whereof tendeth to draw together a greate concourse of loose people.'

The **Henley-in-Arden Heritage Centre** in the High street is housed in a part-14th century building. It describes the history of the town, and includes a model of Beaudesert castle.

Just outside Henley lies **Beaudesert**. This village is even older than its near neighbour Henley and contains a good few timber-framed cottages and the beautifully restored Norman **church of St Nicholas**.

WOTTON WAWEN   Map 2 ref C6
9 miles S of Solihull off the A3400

Handy for walks on nearby Stratford Canal., Wotton Wawen contains some fine timber-framed buildings. Views from the village encompass some outstanding vistas of the surrounding countryside.

The village's name is part Saxon in origin: the suffix *'Wawen'* having been added to distinguish the village from other Wottons, and coming from the Saxon thane who held the land prior to the arrival of the Normans.

Situated in a hollow, the village is dominated by its **church of St Peter** . This impressive structure still has its Saxon tower and stands within a picturesque churchyard which has won the Diocesan 'Best Kept' award several times. The main building is actually three churches in one; there are three completely separate chapels tacked on to each other with a refreshing disregard for architectural design which does not in any way detract from the church's charm.

Next to the church stands **Wotton Hall**, dating from 1637. Maria Fitzherbert, wife of George IV, spent her childhood here and is thought now to return in ghostly form, the *'Grey Lady'* who has been seen wandering about the Hall.

Located within Yew Tree Farm Craft Centre here in Wotton Wawen, **The Heron's Nest** is a cosy and stylish restaurant and tea room occupying a converted barn. Owner Victoria Foster has been in catering for many years and is a first-class cook. Aided by daughter Kristine, she makes a visit to this handsome and comfortable establishment a real treat. The stone floors, exposed brick walls, and exposed ceiling and support beams speak of this building's rich and distinguished past, while Victoria's modern touches add to guests' comfort and pleasure. Visitors can dine on ground level or up in the minstrels' gallery, overlooking a view of the countryside.

The Heron's Nest, Yew Tree Farm Craft Centre, Wotton Wawen Henley in Arden, Warwickshire B95 6BY Tel: 01564 792979.

On fine days, guests are welcome to sit in the lovely, well-tended garden. The menu offers a rich and varied range of traditional favourites, including tempting sandwiches, salads and jacket potatoes, and home-made cakes, all making use of the freshest local ingredients where available. Open: Tuesday to Sunday, 10 a.m.-5 p.m.

STUDLEY
MAP 2 REF C6

8 miles SW of Solihull off the A435

The main road through Studley is the Roman *Rykneild Street* (now the A435). Recorded in the Domesday Book in 1086 as the Saxon 'clearing for horses', it takes its name from the original farmstead hacked to form the edge of the ancient Forest of Arden. Before Henry VIII disagreed with the Pope there was a Priory here; now the place of worship is the church dedicated to the Nativity of the Virgin. It has Norman foundations, and some original features survive the rebuilding that occurred in the 15th century and later. There is also here in Studley an early 18th-century manor house with stone pilasters and columns, protected by striking iron gates.

Just past the Henley-Redditch roundabout, before you reach Mappleborough Green, **Summer Palace Chinese Restaurant** is an unprepossessing and welcoming establishment located on the western border of Warwickshire. This attractive family-run establishment boasts a fine menu of Cantonese and Peking cuisine, from favourites such as aromatic crispy

**Summer Palace Chinese Restaurant, Birmingham Road
Mappleborough Green, Studley, Warwickshire B80 7DF
Tel: 01527 854770/857118.**

duck with pancakes and king prawn chow mein to more innovative choices such as deep fried seaweed and beancurd with sweet and sour sauce. All dishes are home-made and make use of the best and freshest local produce daily. To complement the fine food there is an excellent wine list. Open Monday-Thursday 12-2.30 p.m. and 6-11.30 p.m., Friday-Saturday 12-2.30 p.m. and 6 p.m.-midnight, Sundays 12-2.30 p.m. and 6-11 p.m.

ALCESTER

Alcester is an ancient Roman market town built on the Icknield Street Encampment. It boasts several very pretty cottages on Maltmill Lane and a handsome Norman church. Alcester is popular for good local walks along the confluence of the Rivers Alne and Arrow. The town has been regional winner of a *Britain in Bloom* award.

Owners John and Patricia Brain bring 20 years' catering experience to making **Tudor Rose Tea Rooms and Restaurant** a very pleasant experience. As its name suggests, it occupies a Tudor half-timbered building built in 1512, still with its original ceiling, beams and rare back-to-back Inglenook fireplace. Set back off the High Street behind an antiques shop, just below the Norman church, it affords a welcome haven for a spot of tea and relaxation.

Tudor Rose Tea Rooms and Restaurant, 9a High Street, Alcester Warwickshire B49 5AF Tel: 01789 763025.

The walled patio garden features spring-flowering Kolkwitzia Chinese shrubs, providing good shade in summer, and a mass of hanging baskets and pot plants. The interior is spacious and welcoming, with very comfortable furnishings; the walls are adorned with paintings and prints of local scenes. Traditional breakfasts are served from 9 a.m. til 6 p.m., all-day tea and coffee with freshly made scones, cakes, pies and pastries, and lunch, served from 12 til 5, boasts a fine selection of roast dinners and popular traditional English and vegetarian meals. The home-made puddings are a speciality. John is a mine of information on local scenic walks in the area.

AROUND ALCESTER

COUGHTON   MAP 2 REF C6
2 miles N of Alcester off the A435

The parish church of this very pretty village was built by Sir Robert Throckmorton between 1486 and 1518. It has six bells which were restored in 1976 but are still carried in their original wooden frame. Inside there are some interesting oddments: a faceless clock, fish weather vanes and a dole cupboard from which wheaten loaves were distributed to the needy.

The crowning glory of the village is of course the superb manor house, **Coughton Court.** This mainly Elizabethan house is renowned for its imposing gatehouse and beautiful courtyard. Home of the Throckmorton family since 1409, it is still lived in by the family who built it. The family were very prominent in Tudor times and were instigators of Catholic emancipation, playing a part in the Gunpowder Plot - the wives of some of the Gunpowder Plotters awaited the outcome of the Plot in the central gatehouse.

The house contains one of the best collections of portraits, furniture, porcelain and memorabilia of one family from early Tudor times to the present day. Treasured possessions include the chemise of Mary Queen of Scots and the Throckmorton Coat; the former was worn by Queen Mary at her execution in 1587. The Coat was the subject of a 1,000 guinea wager in 1811. The priest's hole found in the house was constructed by one of the most famous builders of hiding places, Nicholas Owen. The Gunpowder Plot Exhibition highlights the history of the Plot and its connections with the Throckmortons. The Children's Clothes Exhibition features mainly 19th century displays.

This National Trust property has extensive gardens and grounds, lake and two churches to visit. The courtyard shows fine examples of Eliza-

Coughton Court

bethan half-timbering and the recently added knot garden layout. The fountain Pool in the courtyard leads out to formal paths of lime trees. Spring heralds a magnificent display of over 100,000 daffodils and other spring blooms. The grounds also boast a walk planted with willows and native shrubs and trees beside the River Arrow, a new bog garden, a formal orchard and a walled garden project opened in 1996 and maturing into a splendid example of garden 'rooms' set with their own particular plant themes. One herbaceous border is planted with cools blues and yellows, the other with hot reds and orange.

Also on site there is The Tudor Restaurant serving coffee, lunches and teas, an attractive gift shop and a plant centre selling special shrubs, unusual herbaceous plants and a range of herbs, most of them in the gardens here. The magnificent scenery of the Vale of Evesham, the Cotswolds and the Malverns is close by.

ARROW
2 miles S of Alcester off the A422

MAP 2 REF C6

The village of Arrow is interesting to stroll around (despite some development) - as is the pretty stream that divides Arrow and Alcester. Though fruit farming around here is much rarer than it used to be, there are still to be found delicious fresh dessert plums for sale in the late summer and early autumn.

Nearby **Ragley Hall** is a genuine 17th century treasure. The Warwickshire home of the Marquess and Marchioness of Hertford, it is a perfectly symmetrical Palladian house set in 400 acres of parkland and gardens landscaped by Capability Brown. One of England's great Palladian country houses, it was inherited by the eighth Marquess in 1940 when he was only nine. During the Second World War the house was used as a hospital, and thereafter became almost completely derelict. In 1956 the Marquess married, and he and his wife set about making the Hall their home. All the main rooms have been redecorated in colours similar to the original ones that would have been used, and the process of restoring and improving continues. Today, with all the interest generated in 17th century style and taste generated by the popularity of the works of Jane Austen as depicted in several television series, a lasting interest and enthusiasm for this 18th century microcosm would seem to be ensured.

This magnificent stately home boasts James Gibb's elegant Baroque plasterwork in the Great Hall, as well as Graham Rust's stunning 20th century mural, 'The Temptation'. A tour takes in Ragley Hall's fabulous collection of treasures from a bygone age, featuring paintings (including

Ragley Hall

some modern art), china, furniture and a goodly assortment of Victorian and Edwardian dolls and toys. The Stables house an impressive carriage collection.

The main formal garden, to the west of the Hall, descends in a series of wide terraces, now entirely occupied by roses. The rest of the garden, covering 24 acres, consists of shrubs and trees interspersed with spacious lawns providing vistas across the 400 acre park. The lake, created in 1625, is now used for fishing, sailing, swimming and water skiing; there is also a lakeside picnic area. The cricket pitch is in regular use. A country trail of about two miles wends its way through the park and the woods, to end at a very popular adventure playground.

The Hall also boasts licensed terrace tea rooms. Special events such as craft fairs, gardeners' weekends, dog trials and outdoor concerts are held throughout the year.

Just opposite the entrance to Ragley Hall, **The Arrow Mill Hotel** is a distinctive and picturesque hotel occupying a former working (and famous) flour mill mentioned in the Domesday Book - where it was valued at 3s 6d! - and set in lovely grounds astride the mill pool which runs to the River Arrow, a tributary of the River Avon. The 18 guest rooms are individually decorated with great taste and style. Owners Simon and Agnes Woodhams are deservedly proud of this handsome establishment, and work hard to keep up its reputation for service and attention to detail. Simon, a fully-qualified chef, supervises the international kitchen staff. The restaurant overlooks the mill pool and river, and offers a full a la carte menu as well

The Arrow Mill Hotel, Arrow, Nr Alcester, Warwickshire B49 5NL
Tel: 01789 762419 Fax: 01789 765170.

as bar snacks. All dishes make use of fresh local produce in carefully created dishes - encompassing the full range from traditional to more innovative choices. The excellent food can be washed down with any of the selection of real ales - including a local ale from the Fat Gods Brewery a mile down the road - and extensive choice of wines on offer.

The county's best drive, which takes in part of Gloucestershire, circles Alcester, via Walcote, Aston Cantlow, Wilmcote, Temple Grafton, Wixford, Radford, Inkberrow, Holberrow Green, New End and Kings Coughton.

EXHALL   MAP 2 REF C7
2 miles SE of Alcester off the A46

South of the A46, where there is a marked trail through the woods at Oversley, visitors will come to Exhall, recorded in the Domesday Book though its history probably dates back to Roman times. Roman coins have been found in one of the village gardens. The architecture in this handsome village is varied, reflecting the history and development from Elizabethan to modern times. The village is also home to some interesting black-and-white half-timbered buildings and a farmhouse dating back to the 16th century. Most of the houses stand on steep banks on each side of the road, and this adds much to the picturesque quality of the village. The parish **church of St Giles** has a fine Norman door; the views from the churchyard are beautiful.

DUNNINGTON   MAP 2 REF C7
3 miles SW of Alcester off the B4088

The Hiller Garden and Dunnington Heath Farm is a two acre garden with all-year-round interest displaying unusual herbaceous perennials, old-fashioned and species roses, and English roses, open as part of the charitable National Gardens Scheme. Cream teas available.

BROOM   MAP 2 REF C7
3 miles S of Alcester off the A46

This attractive village boasts some handsome black-and-white Tudor buildings, including **Broom Hall Inn**, which dates back in its oldest parts to 1577. The Hall was formerly a farmhouse.

MARLCLIFF   MAP 2 REF C7
5 miles S of Alcester off the B4085

The River Avon runs right through this delightful village, set near Cleeve Hill Ridge and Reserve. **Woodpeckers** is a distinguished two-and-a-half acre plantsman's country garden designed and maintained with care and style. Incorporating colour-schemed borders, old roses, a meadow garden, small arboretum, alpines grown in troughs and gravel, a pool, Tudor-style knot garden and potager, it has been featured on BBC2's Gardener's World and in The English Garden and The Garden. Visitors welcome at all seasons, please telephone 01789 773416 for details.

WIXFORD
3 miles S of Alcester off the B4085

MAP 2 REF C7

This pretty village on the River Arrow lies at the edge of the Vale of Evesham, just five minutes away from Ragley Hall and Bidford-on-Avon. It boasts a famous local church.

The Three Horseshoes is a charming and convivial family-run pub with a rich history. The interior of this warm and welcoming pub boasts an old forge and is adorned with old photos, clippings and mementos of local interest; there is also an interesting collection of working forge implements. The two dining rooms, one earmarked for families, are spacious and comfortable. There's an extensive choice of real ales and wines, and a

The Three Horseshoes, Wixford, Nr Alcester, Warwickshire B49 6DG
Tel: 01789 490400.

choice of bar snacks and grills, as well as a daily menu of freshly prepared home-cooked meals, with imaginative dishes, traditional favourites and a large vegetarian selection - and a range of wonderful puddings. There are two patio areas, children's play area and lovely gardens with a fine display of flowers all year round, as befits former winners of the National Pub Gardens Award.

WELFORD-ON-AVON
5 miles SE of Alcester off the B439

MAP 2 REF C7

The village of Welford-on-Avon boasts many pretty half-timbered cottages and a famous Maypole on the village green - the local festival of Maypole and Morris dancing is held in July each year. This village, at the outer reaches of 'The Greenway' from Stratford, is popular but well away from the hub-bub of busy centres such as Stratford and Warwick.

The Shakespeare pub occupies a listed late 18th century building in the heart of this charming village alongside the river Avon. The interior has been refurbished recently but retains the original stone flagstones and open log fires. Most of the furniture has been hand-made by local craftsmen. An old well has pride of place in the pub, and a collection of artwork

**The Shakespeare, Welford on Avon, Warwickshire CV37 8PX
Tel: 01789 750443.**

by local artists adorns the walls. Another unique feature is the collection of over 2,000 paperback books - customers can borrow any they fancy for a few days. Owners Philip and Jenny Tormey are friendly hosts; Jenny is particularly knowledgeable about the long history and traditions of the pub, village and surrounding area. The lovely rear garden has won the *Best Pub Garden award*. There is a fine selection of real ales on offer, as well as a wide range of house reds and whites, and over 40 malt whiskies. A wide range of food is freshly prepared and cooked from local produce - the steak and kidney pie is a speciality, as are the great puddings.

CLIFFORD CHAMBERS

MAP 2 REF D7

6 miles SE of Alcester off the B439

Clifford Chambers has attractive timbered houses and a Tudor rectory which some claim was the true birthplace of William Shakespeare.

The excellent **Shire Horse Centre** features parades and demonstrations of these huge beasts, as well as areas devoted to goats, pigs and rare breeds, an owl sanctuary with falconry displays and an adventure playground.

LOWER QUINTON

MAP 2 REF D7

7 miles SE of Alcester off the B4632

This village has black-and-white Cotswold cottages and a picturesque village green. Two miles from the Gloucestershire border, just below the Cotswold hills, **The Say Dog** is a warm and welcoming public house with a relaxed atmosphere. Set amidst lovely countryside, affording some interesting walks along the edge of the Cotswolds, this late 17th century former farmhouse, then gentlemen's club, was owned in the 1920s and 30s by a famous breeder of spaniels and Crufts judge - hence the pub's unusual name, one of only two left in the country. It hearkens back to a long tradition of unspoilt country pubs, with three small rooms as well as a larger lounge, and a skittle alley in a separate outbuilding. The menu is

**The Say Dog, Friday Street, Lower Quinton, Nr Stratford-upon-Avon
Warwickshire CV37 8SK Tel: 01789 720237.**

extensive, the range of choices all home-cooked and freshly prepared. The portions are generous, and house specialities include Sunday roast beef and pork dishes, and the locally renowned mixed grill. There is also a wide choice of real ales and ciders, as well as a good selection of wines.

LONG MARSTON
6 miles SE of Alcester off the B4632

MAP 2 REF C7

Charles I stayed at a house here in Long Marston after his flight from the Battle of Worcester. The village's 14th-century church has a half-timbered turret and porch.

From Long Marston there's access to **The Greenway**, a converted railway line ideal for cycling or walking. This open public greensward boasts two and a half miles of surfaced paths amid beautiful scenery, with picnic areas and a tranquil atmosphere of rural calm.

ILMINGTON
9 miles SE of Alcester off the B4632

MAP 2 REF D8

Along the northeastern Cotswolds, at the foot of the Wilmington Downs, you'll come to the village of Ilmington. This eye-catching place has several lovely old houses. Its part-Norman church, which features oak furnishings by Robert Thompson of Yorkshire, is approached through a Norman arch. This is truly a hidden place and one of the most picturesque one could hope to find. Lying in the valley between the Campden and Foxcote hills, it is surrounded by green fields and Cotswold countryside. Here there are fine old stone cottages with roses round the doors, and gardens full of colour.

The village's name means 'the elm grown hill'. It was made famous on Christmas Day 1934, when the first radio broadcast by George V was introduced by Walton Handy, the village shepherd, and relayed to the world from **Ilmington Manor**, the fine Elizabethan house once owned by the De Montfort family. The remains of a tramway, once the main form of transport to the village, can still be seen.

The nearby Ilmington Downs are, at 850 feet, the highest point in the county, commanding fine views of the surrounding country.

Across the B4632 you will pass Meon Hill, where an Iron Age fort stood dominating the valley.

TOURIST
INFORMATION
CENTRES

Centres in **bold** are open all the year around.

Birmingham Tourist Information Centres

Convention and Visitor Bureau, 2 City Arcade, Birmingham
West Midlands, B2 4TX
Tel No: 0121 643 2514 Fax No: 0121 616 1038

Convention and Visitor Bureau, National Exhibition Centre
Birmingham, West Midlands, B40 1NT
Tel No: 0121 780 4321 Fax No: 0121 780 4260

Visitor Information Centre, 130 Colmore Row, Birmingham
West Midlands, B3 3AP
Tel No: 0121 693 6300 Fax No: 0121 693 9600

Coventry Tourist Information Centre
Bayley Lane, Coventry, West Midlands, CV1 5RN
Tel No: 01203 832303/832304 Fax No: 01203 832370

Dudley Tourist Information Centre
30 Churchill Centre, Dudley, West Midlands, DY2 7BL
Tel No: 01384 812830 Fax No: 01384 815580

Kenilworth Tourist Information Centre
The Library, 11 Smalley Place, Kenilworth, Warwickshire, CV8 1QG
Tel No: 01926 852595 Fax No: 01926 864503

Leamington Spa Tourist Information Centre
Jephson Lodge, Jephson Gardens, The Parade, Royal Leamington Spa
Warwickshire, CV32 4AB
Tel No: 01926 311470 Fax No: 01926 881639

Nuneaton Tourist Information Centre
Nuneaton Library, Church Street, Nuneaton, Warwickshire, CV11 4DR
Tel No: 01203 347006 Fax No: 01203 350125

Rugby Tourist Information Centre
The Library, Little Elborow Street, Rugby, Warwickshire, CV21 3BZ
Tel No: 01788 571813 Fax No: 01788 573289

Solihull Tourist Information Centre
Central Library, Homer Road, Solihull, West Midlands, B91 3RG
Tel No: 0121 704 6130/6134 Fax No: 0121 704 6991

Stratford Tourist Information Centre
Bridgefoot, Stratford-upon-Avon, Warwickshire, CV37 6GW
Tel No: 01789 293127 Fax No: 01789 295262

Warwick Tourist Information Centre
The Court House, Jury Street, Warwick, Warwickshire, CV34 4EW
Tel No: 01926 492212 Fax No: 01926 494837

INDEX OF TOWNS
AND VILLAGES

INDEX OF PLACES TO STAY, EAT, DRINK & SHOP

Chapter 4: Central Warwickshire

Chapter 5: Stratford-upon-Avon & South Warwickshire

Chapter 6: Solihull and Southwestern Warwickshire

INDEX OF PLACES OF INTEREST

THE HIDDEN PLACES
——— Order Form ———

To order any of our publications just fill in the payment details below and complete the order form *overleaf*. For orders of less than 4 copies please add £1 per book for postage and packing. Orders over 4 copies are P & P free.

Please Complete Either:

I enclose a cheque for £ .... made payable to Travel Publishing Ltd

Or:

Card No: ☐☐☐☐ ☐☐☐☐ ☐☐☐☐ ☐☐☐☐

Expiry Date: ☐☐ ☐☐

Signature: ....

NAME: ....

ADDRESS: ....

....

....

POSTCODE: ....

TEL NO: ....

Please send to: Travel Publishing Ltd
7a Apollo House
Calleva Park
Aldermaston
Berks, RG7 8TN

THE HIDDEN PLACES
Order Form

	Price	Quantity	Value
Regional Titles			
Cambridgeshire & Lincolnshire	£7.99	....	....
Channel Islands	£6.99	....	....
Cheshire	£7.99	....	....
Cornwall	£7.99	....	....
Devon	£7.99	....	....
Dorset, Hants & Isle of Wight	£4.95	....	....
Essex	£7.99	....	....
Gloucestershire	£6.99	....	....
Heart of England	£4.95	....	....
Highlands & Islands	£7.99	....	....
Kent	£7.99	....	....
Lake District & Cumbria	£7.99	....	....
Lancashire	£7.99	....	....
Norfolk	£7.99	....	....
Northeast Yorkshire	£6.99	....	....
Northumberland & Durham	£6.99	....	....
North Wales	£7.99	....	....
Nottinghamshire	£6.99	....	....
Peak District	£6.99	....	....
Potteries	£6.99	....	....
Somerset	£6.99	....	....
South Wales	£4.95	....	....
Suffolk	£7.99	....	....
Surrey	£6.99	....	....
Sussex	£6.99	....	....
Thames & Chilterns	£5.99	....	....
Warwickshire & West Midlands	£7.99	....	....
Welsh Borders	£5.99	....	....
Wiltshire	£6.99	....	....
Yorkshire Dales	£6.99	....	....
Set of any 5 Regional titles	**£25.00**	....	....
National Titles			
England	£9.99	....	....
Ireland	£8.99	....	....
Scotland	£8.99	....	....
Wales	£8.99	....	....
Set of all 4 National titles	**£28.00**	....	....

For orders of less than 4 copies please add £1 per book for postage & packing. Orders over 4 copies P & P free.

THE HIDDEN PLACES
—— Reader Comment Form ——

The *Hidden Places* research team would like to receive reader's comments on any visitor attractions or places reviewed in the book and also recommendations for suitable entries to be included in the next edition. This will help ensure that the *Hidden Places* series continues to provide its readers with useful information on the more interesting, unusual or unique features of each attraction or place ensuring that their stay in the local area is an enjoyable and stimulating experience.

    To provide your comments or recommendations would you please complete the forms below and overleaf as indicated and send to: The Research Department, Travel Publishing Ltd., 7a Apollo House, Calleva Park, Aldermaston, Reading, RG7 8TN.

Your Name:

Your Address:

Your Telephone Number:

Please tick as appropriate: Comments ☐ Recommendation ☐

Name of *"Hidden Place"*:

Address:

Telephone Number:

Name of Contact:

THE HIDDEN PLACES
—— Reader Comment Form ——

Comment or Reason for Recommendation:

....

....

....

....

....

....

....

....

....

....

....

....

THE HIDDEN PLACES
—— Reader Comment Form ——

The *Hidden Places* research team would like to receive reader's comments on any visitor attractions or places reviewed in the book and also recommendations for suitable entries to be included in the next edition. This will help ensure that the *Hidden Places* series continues to provide its readers with useful information on the more interesting, unusual or unique features of each attraction or place ensuring that their stay in the local area is an enjoyable and stimulating experience.

To provide your comments or recommendations would you please complete the forms below and overleaf as indicated and send to: The Research Department, Travel Publishing Ltd., 7a Apollo House, Calleva Park, Aldermaston, Reading, RG7 8TN.

Your Name:

Your Address:

Your Telephone Number:

Please tick as appropriate: Comments ☐ Recommendation ☐

Name of *"Hidden Place"*:

Address:

Telephone Number:

Name of Contact:

THE HIDDEN PLACES
—— Reader Comment Form ——

Comment or Reason for Recommendation:

....

....

....

....

....

....

....

....

....

....

....

....

T H E   H I D D E N   P L A C E S
—— Reader Comment Form ——

The *Hidden Places* research team would like to receive reader's comments on any visitor attractions or places reviewed in the book and also recommendations for suitable entries to be included in the next edition. This will help ensure that the *Hidden Places* series continues to provide its readers with useful information on the more interesting, unusual or unique features of each attraction or place ensuring that their stay in the local area is an enjoyable and stimulating experience.

To provide your comments or recommendations would you please complete the forms below and overleaf as indicated and send to: The Research Department, Travel Publishing Ltd., 7a Apollo House, Calleva Park, Aldermaston, Reading, RG7 8TN.

Your Name:

Your Address:

Your Telephone Number:

Please tick as appropriate: Comments ☐   Recommendation ☐

Name of *"Hidden Place"*:

Address:

Telephone Number:

Name of Contact:

THE HIDDEN PLACES
—— Reader Comment Form ——

Comment or Reason for Recommendation:

....

....

....

....

....

....

....

....

....

....

....

....

MAP SECTION

The following pages of maps encompass the main cities, towns and geographical features of Warwickshire and The West Midlands, as well as many of the interesting places featured in the guide. Distances are indicated by the use of scale bars located below each of the maps

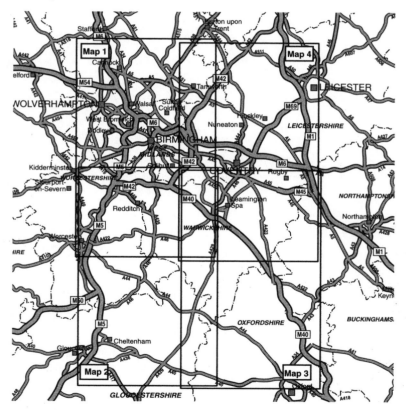

Map 1

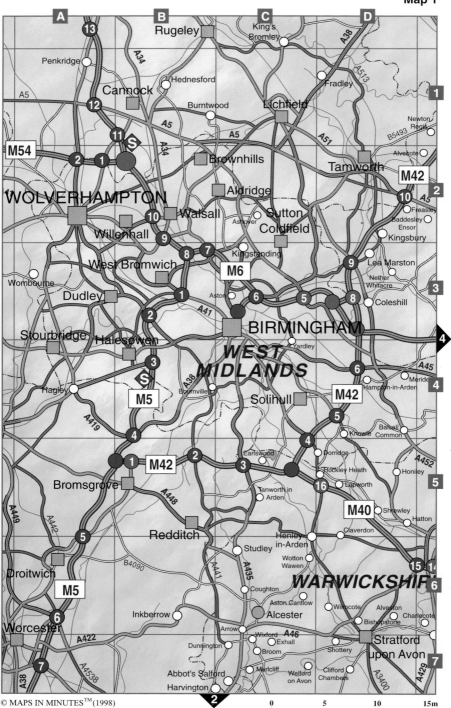

© MAPS IN MINUTES™ (1998)

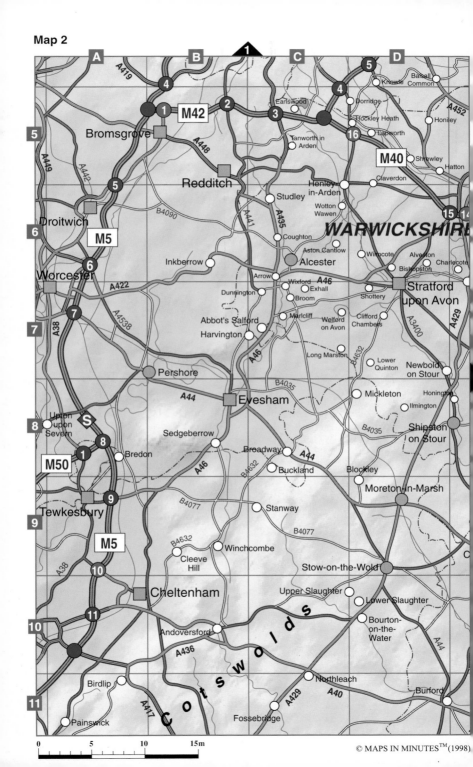

Map 2

© MAPS IN MINUTES™ (1998)